TAKE OFF
THE
MASKS

TAKE OFF THE MASKS

THE CLASSIC SPIRITUAL AUTOBIOGRAPHY

REVISED WITH A NEW EPILOGUE

MALCOLM BOYD

HarperSanFrancisco
A Division of HarperCollins*Publishers*

The stories in this book are true; however, to protect the privacy of individuals involved, certain names, dates, places, and likenesses have been altered.

Copyright acknowledgments can be found on page 207.

TAKE OFF THE MASKS. Copyright © 1978 by Malcolm Boyd. Revised edition copyright © 1993 by Malcolm Boyd. All rights reserved. Printed in the United States of America. No part of this book may be used or reproduced in any manner whatsoever without written permission except in the case of brief quotations embodied in critical articles and reviews. For information address HarperCollins Publishers, 10 East 53rd Street, New York, NY 10022.

REVISED HARPERCOLLINS PAPERBACK EDITION PUBLISHED IN 1993.

Library of Congress Cataloging-in-Publication Data

Boyd, Malcolm.
Take off the masks : the classic spiritual autobiography : revised, with a new epilogue / Malcolm Boyd.
    p.   cm.
ISBN 0–06–060863–3
1. Boyd, Malcolm. 2. Episcopal Church—Clergy—Biography.
3. Anglican Communion—United States—Clergy—Biography.
4. Gays—United States—Biography. I. Title.
BX5995.B66A37 1993   91–53901
305.38'9664'092—dc20   CIP

93 94 95 96 97 ❖ RRD(H) 10 9 8 7 6 5 4 3 2 1

This edition is printed on acid-free paper that meets the American National Standards Institute Z39.48 Standard.

To Mark Thompson

Contents

Introduction

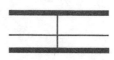

I

If we do not understand history, we risk having to repeat it. My story in this book is one of a long-hidden homosexual life prior to coming out and discovering myself as a gay man.

Who would wish that on anyone—the years in a straitjacket? Thank God they're over. Yet they happened. I think it is important to know what they were, how they occurred, when and where life's details emerged, and why all this was apparently necessary.

This is the intimate account of one man who lived long years before Stonewall. It is not the story of a Harry Hay or Harvey Milk, an out-of-the-closet gay liberationist fighter and hero. Instead it is the chronicle of a gay man who was long inside the closet, struggling to get out and affirm humanity. Probably there are more gay men and lesbians like me than the celebrated ongoing heroes.

To some young gay men and lesbians my story might seem as remote as one out of the Ming dynasty. I hope not. Because it's a real, flesh-and-blood, fairly contemporary account, and there are hundreds, even thousands, that resemble it. Let's not reject our history. It is essential to integrate it into all our lives as a gay people.

Nothing can separate us from the love of God. It took me seemingly forever to learn this, know it in my bones, enflesh it, get it moving in my bloodstream. Love can touch us even when we don't realize it. The power of love is stronger than any other power.

Let me share something with you from my own life. As a young gay boy growing up, I was so scared. I felt utterly alone, alien, unattractive. Hardly anybody apparently loved me; if *they* found out the truth about me, *nobody* would. All I had were my books, the opera broadcasts on Saturdays, and my fantasies and dreams of a beautiful world that awaited me somewhere.

I was in high school and had a special friend, Virginia. She was older, a student in med school. Why was she so nice to me? Why did she find time for me? She was sophisticated and sure of herself, drove a red convertible, went to bars, had black friends, and said clever things that got quoted.

Virginia would pick me up in her convertible and take me to the Pencol drugstore for a Coke. The Pencol was where the beautiful people went for a Coke. Virginia wasn't ashamed of me. I couldn't figure it out because I was so unattractive and unsure of myself in high school.

Sometimes I visited Virginia at home. She wore pants with her shirttail out and had lots of records. I played "The Man I Love." I remember when she got kicked out of med school; they said it was because she was a lesbian.

I grew up, went away to school, and didn't come back to live. But I visited once ten years later. Virginia was still so sophisticated, so beautiful, so kind. She still loved me. She took my hand in hers, held it, and said it was a lovely hand. She knew a man who would love to know me. I was scared. I wanted to say yes, but said no.

Years passed, and I returned a last time to visit Virginia. She had had a stroke, spoke with difficulty, and walked with a cane. Virginia's old family home had once been aristocratic and in the best part of town. Now it was in a slum. A bottle of milk or a newspaper left on the front porch was stolen unless picked up right away. On that porch on my last night Virginia gave a dinner party for me. There was a card table. A fancy, faded tablecloth. The old, good silver. Candlelight. Virginia. A lesbian nurse, an old lover of hers. A lesbian army sergeant, an old lover of hers. And me. It was a glorious dinner; we laughed and cried. Tennessee Williams would have loved it. Geraldine Page could have played it. The next morning I left. The next year I heard Virginia had died.

Virginia's coming into my life meant that I knew the meaning of love as a young gay boy who was scared and alone. There were no gay role models, lesbian or gay newspapers or magazines, well-known artists or athletes who were out. The word *homosexual* was a whispered curse. *Queer* was worse. The story of the Exodus in the Bible is, it seems to me, very much our story as gay people. The Passover Seder in Judaism is based on it. It has five stages. The first is slavery. We have all known it: racism, sexism, homophobia, prejudice, stereotyping, paternalistic myths. Virtually all of us have been victims of fundamentalistic, Khomeini-like hate. Margaret Atwood's novel *A Handmaid's Tale* reveals graphically and explicitly the kind of world and the sort of twisted society that are the natural outgrowth of a fundamentalist vision of the world, God, and human life.

The second stage of the Passover Seder is a response to slavery. A refusal to remain a slave. Coming out. Making a decision to live, love, pursue happiness, and become fulfilled.

The third stage is to confront Pharaoh. This means standing up and saying "Enough!" to censorship, idolatry, authoritarianism, enemies of freedom, and fear and loathing of the human body and life. A corollary of this is to say "Yes!" to love, nurturing, feeding, and liberation.

The fourth step is, after confronting Pharaoh, to wander in the wilderness. How well we know the wilderness. We search for identity, love, relationship, and freedom.

Finally, we come to the fifth and final stage of the Passover Seder: arrival at home. A sense of community. Creative, life-affirming connections. The realization that neither death nor life can separate us from the love of God. In our keen awareness of arrival, we place our feet on a mountaintop and look out to see the promised land.

Problems are not insurmountable; they have solutions. Instead of being overwhelmed, we can take a tip from the twelve-step program of Alcoholics Anonymous and approach the big picture a step at a time and give up the illusion of control and let a greater power assert love and peace in our life.

Why am I gay?

No one can really explain it to me.

Yes, I like to have sex with members of my own sex.

Yes, I have yearned forever for what was mysteriously and stubbornly called forbidden fruit.

Yes, I have fought and struggled, tooth and nail, against the tyranny that would kill my nature—mercilessly changing me into a vegetable, albeit a socially acceptable one.

I'm tired of Bible-spouting hypocrites who talk about love in God's name while they hate my sisters and brothers—and me.

I'm sick of self-righteous inquisitors who quote Scripture even while they light the faggots to burn, turn the screw of the rack to draw more blood and screams, and hammer nails into countless bodies on numberless crosses in order to murder the human spirit.

At long last I have come to know myself as free. I have taken off my mask, and the sun and rain upon my naked face feel marvelous. The mystery of my gayness I celebrate with joy and thanksgiving.

Thank you, God, for making me gay.

1993

II

My chalk-white clown's face was punctuated by black crow's-foot wrinkles at the outer corners of my eyes, bright red lips, and orange hearts painted on my cheeks when I played the role of a clown one Sunday morning in New York City in the spring of 1977.

Wearing greasepaint, I became someone else as I stepped into my clown's costume. Automatically I was required to play a role even beyond the one I am usually asked to play on the stage of my life.

Several months earlier I had revealed to the world that I am gay. A newsmagazine described how many had viewed me—"blunt, restless, eloquent, and above all, open." Yet it noted the brooding presence of a mask in my public life: "He kept one aspect of his life deeply private: his homosexuality."

I kept my homosexuality so private that originally I planned to write this book to be published posthumously. Finally I have come to accept my place as among the living. Now I want to engage in whatever debate or controversy may surround the book. Yet why is there controversy? Why isn't my gayness, and that of others, accepted as a normal sexual orientation and behavior for millions of gay people?

A deeper question is that of forced conformity to arbitrary cultural norms. I will not play an assigned role that dishonors the integrity of my being. I do not want to inflict hurt on loved ones or close friends who may perhaps never be able to understand. Yet I cannot continue to commit the slow suicide of negating life. I have decided to assert my God-given humanity.

I can no longer tolerate not being able to be myself. Gayness is my ethnicity. Can't I really be known in the full dimension of who I am?

This has been in some ways a painful book to write, yes, but also a liberating, affirming, and—finally—happy one. Writing it has had a profound, disturbing, but deeply freeing effect on my own life. You see, it means taking a lantern and casting bright light into what was a forbidden dungeon of my life.

At first, and for most of the years in my life, I knew myself to be a "queer," not a proud affirmation as it is now, but a crippling condemnation. That is what society and the church scrupulously taught me I was. The conclusion was very clear: hide. Hide inside a dark closet and never step outside unless you wear a socially acceptable mask that obscures your truth and is therefore a lie. Live a lie.

Later I came to understand that I had moved up the social ladder to become a "homosexual." I had crept outside the shadows of utter shame and degradation and now had become a statistic that was mentioned in polite society—as an example of mental sickness, spiritual sin, public shame, and private hell.

As a "queer" and a "homosexual" I had to play roles that did not let my person outside an airless, sad prison. In this book I want to place these roles on stage for the last time and let the curtain fall on them. For now I know that I am a gay person—whole, healthy, blessed, happy, created in God's own image, and free of the past horrors of human slavery.

How did such a fundamental change take place in my life? There was no twinkling moment of miracle, but instead slow, gradual change, as this book explains. I remember sitting in a darkened theater several years ago and watching the film *Sunday, Bloody Sunday.* My God, there was my hidden self, right up there on that massive screen! I watched the casual interplay between gays that was part of my most intimate experience. I heard the gasps and titters in the audience as the two men kissed.

When the film came to its bitter ending, tears flooded my eyes and poured down my cheeks. The house lights came up. I did not wish to walk out amid laughing and brightly talking people while I was crying. Brushing against the crowd, I made my way to the front of the theater, hurried out a door marked "Exit," and found myself outside on a fire escape. Alone, now, and blinking back the tears, I climbed down to the alley below.

Immediately I realized the cause of my acute pain. I had just seen images of wholly unnecessary sadness and pain. Enough! I said. I knew that if I lived in a society that did not repress or condemn so much of human sexuality, including homosexuality, my life could have been a much happier and freer one. However, I decided henceforth to make positive sense out of my life's experience as a gay person.

First, I would have to shut off all the escape valves, face myself, and confront my demons. Soon I withdrew steadily from the activist-celebrity orbit. Healing began. Humor reasserted itself, as did human perspective. Deliberately I let numerous spaces in my life remain empty for the time being, so that I could gradually flex my life's muscles and learn to move easily and simply.

I made a resolution. Whenever society made a totalitarian demand upon me to conform to its script or stage directions, makeup requirements, or public relations orders, I would refuse. To fit securely into an acceptable image, speak on cue, play a given role, and finally die after tragically honoring society's dictates to the finale: *No!* I learned that I could peel off my costuming, all the way down to my naked skin. Slowly, slowly it dawned upon me that grace and love are synonymous, as are grace and freedom.

I deeply needed to comprehend this truth. Following the publication of *Are You Running with Me, Jesus?* I had become a celebrity. This intensified the dichotomy between my public and private "lives." Earlier I had been a Freedom Rider and participated in scores of demonstrations in the South and North for the freedom of black people, incurring frequent arrests. I was arrested twice inside the Pentagon and once across from the White House while demonstrating nonviolently for peace and against the undeclared U.S. war in Vietnam. I publicly affirmed my support of the ordination of women priests and wrote a *Ms.* cover story entitled "Who's Afraid of Women Priests—and Why They Won't Admit It." On two successive Christmas Eve occasions I led a Christian pilgrimage to Jerusalem's Western ("Wailing") Wall, the holiest site of Judaism, to offer thanks publicly for the Jewishness of Jesus, express penitence for Christian involvement in Jewish persecution, and call for a new spiritual covenant between Christians and the Jewish people.

Yet I had found no way that I might ever know a depth of freedom in my own gay experience. I felt utterly trapped. For the sake of the church, I had long endeavored to conform to its professional expectations by hiding the reality of my being. Somehow, I told myself, I would maintain the correct image. But then I beheld its own professionalism at war against the will of God. The church remained racist—regard the churchly blessing of segregated housing patterns, the apartheid maintenance of private church-operated schools for white students, and the tokenistic employment of minority clergy. The church maintained a stunning establishment silence during the Vietnam War. It has long placed its endowments and real estate interests ahead of the crying needs of poor people. It has betrayed countless people in sexuality, causing untold suffering when it broke human beings against the harsh strictures of stony legalism.

I was deeply in love on three different occasions when I knew myself as a "queer" and a "homosexual." In none of these cases was there any way for us to build a relationship by living openly together with any permanence or peace, due to social anger and churchly condemnation. The fire that burned in me on these occasions could not be extinguished by alcohol, tears, or semen. The fire had to burn itself out. I asked myself: Instead of maintaining a double standard for gay people, why doesn't society permit an honest public legitimization of relations between consenting adults as well as of gay civil rights?

Let me explain here that I cannot recall a sexual relationship that was ever simply casual for me. Always I felt an intensity, a yearning to belong and love, and an awesome sense of universal meaning in *this* act. Surely this has brought me sadness as well as joy. I stood outside as well as inside each relationship. I could never dismiss it easily, just let it go, say it was "nice." A sense of belonging and home somehow always eluded me; I seemed to be incapable of completeness. I felt a deep need to belong.

Terrible cries were rigidly contained inside me:

I want . . . I want to love . . . I need to share . . . Take my hand . . . Hold me . . . Come to me . . . Let me come to you . . . Please let me sleep gently with my head on your chest . . . Let me hold my face lovingly in your hair . . . Can we cry and let out all the cries in the world that seem locked inside our bodies? Can we laugh and hold hands in public and kiss softly on the mouth? . . . Finally there are no words, here are our bodies and souls, here is this pent-up love that is deep and beautiful . . . I want to give it, take it, share.

Finally I was overwhelmed by the impossibility of going on forever in a dehumanized mockery of life. It meant subterfuge, guilt, hypocrisy, and the absence of openness. It was even, I profoundly realized, a denial of Jesus Christ. But what could I do? For a long while I withdrew into myself. I would place my work first, indeed, make it my whole life. I tried to sublimate my feelings and live utterly without sexual, physical love. Yet I needed desperately to make sense of my sexuality and capacity to love and relate my fragmented, privatized experience to a universal human one. I wondered: How could I ever achieve wholeness and full personhood, combining my sexuality and spirituality?

Here I am revealing a wholly new aspect of my life to many readers as well as people who have known me simply as a public image. Surely there was a convenient image for labeling and filing me: the religious figure, an activist of the sixties and best-selling author of prayer poems, the "nightclub priest" who read from his work in San Francisco's legendary hungry i.

I am someone else also. There is far more to me than the glibly convenient stereotyped public image. This is not to say that what I did was false. It was not. But I couldn't, I believed, be known in my fullness. Only as I moved gradually away from self-hatred as a "queer" and a "homosexual" toward an understanding and acceptance of myself as a whole person who is gay did I grow and mature as a human being. It is this experience that I want to share with you.

Always I had a sense of my intrinsic worth; society, even labeling me as a "queer," could not take it away. Always I had an awareness of my creation in God's image. I am enormously proud, happy, and grateful to be gay—to be myself. I have survived. I am changing, evolving, and struggling. Now I want to find out where I am going next, who I shall become. I pray for love to be built into my unified private and public life and to realize the fullest potential in myself of what gay, and human, really means. I have no more room in my life for neurotic, gnawing, destructive loneliness. I want all my relationships to possess an intensity that comes only from honesty. In turn, this permits (I have found) a refreshing, unambiguous commitment to our common human experience and its transcendence in the living God.

I do not *ask* for my right to life, liberty, and the pursuit of happiness in what will inevitably be the final years of my life. This right belongs to me. I claim it.

13

For anyone who knows what it is to wear a heavy, stultifying, and imprisoning mask in life, I write this book. I offer my witness. Let's take off the masks.

1978

LIFE IN
THE CLOSET

PART ONE

An Emerging Sexual Consciousness

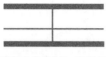

CHAPTER ONE

Childhood

When I was born, my parents engaged Evangeline Adams, known as the high priestess of astrology, to prepare my horoscope on the basis of the positions of the planets at the exact time of my birth. In light of my later awareness of being gay, I find Ms. Adams's predictions in the thirty-five-page horoscope fascinating:

"Be sure that he is not made to feel that he is 'queer,' but rather that he has gifts and possibilities that, if used to advantage, will make him a very superior person."

Again: "Men, beginning with his father, will play a strange part in his destiny and eventually go out either by a misunderstanding or accidental and unexpected death. Older or eccentric men may seem to fascinate him, and, if so, be sure that they are worthy of his confidence and devotion.

"Even as a young child, he should be trained to be conventional, both in the selection of his friends and pleasures, as he may just naturally be attracted by amusements that might be considered questionable.

"His inner desires will be of so unusual a character that he will find it difficult to enjoy the average person, and he may find it difficult to express much that he feels and desires. He may be obliged to masquerade or play a part when in the company of many. He may, for some reason, be forced to associate clandestinely with those who do really understand his nature. Many secrets will seem to touch his life."

My childhood in New York City was a lonely one. As governesses kept me company, walking with me when I tricycled around the great reservoir in Central Park, I yearned for masculine love and company. But I was an only child, and in the late 1920s my father was a busy man. He was the head of a corporate accounting firm that served a lot of import-export companies headquartered in downtown New York. My father was lean, restless, imaginative, warm, an elegant man who was also tough, and he had a touch of the performer about him that I guess I have inherited. He radiated confidence, and he must have been a godsend to companies that were trying to figure out ever more ingenious ways to make money hand over fist. That, in the twenties, seemed to be the National Purpose, and my father was well rewarded for his contribution to that purpose. He earned—and spent on limousines, clothes, parties, all the basics of the sweet life. And I was left much of the time with servants.

My father liked his liquor. But he did most of his serious drinking away from home. He disappeared for a week, two weeks, and took a hotel suite in the city for partying. When he did not drink—most of the time when he went with my mother to parties with their friends—he was a charming man, great fun to be with. Often my parents were away in the evenings, dining at the Waldorf or the Astor, attending the Ziegfeld Follies or the Broadway theater, and afterward stopping off at a favorite club.

But when they entertained guests at home, I was allowed to go into the dining room after my nurse got me ready for bed to say goodnight to my mother and father. Those were the times I looked forward to, because, climbing up and settling in my father's lap, I could play a stalling game about going to bed. My father would smell of cigarettes and bay rum. His face was lined and strong, with just a trace of end-of-the-day stubble. I liked to run my finger across the roughness of his cheek and wonder if someday I would have hair like that. I liked the way his hands held me. I'd look down at the veins and muscles and the shape of the bones, the fingernails, always so cleaned and polished, and despair that my hands would ever be as beautiful as that.

Those were the quiet evenings. Other evenings were not so quiet. Those were the times when my parents would give large parties. No sitting on my father's lap and listening to the radio those evenings. I was hustled into bed and the door to my bedroom was firmly shut. But I had ears. I could listen. To all the talk. The gales of laughter. The blasts of music. The thump of dancing feet and the tinkle of ice in glasses. I'd lie there in the darkness and feel very lonely. Everyone else but me was having a good time. I yearned to grow up, but could I grow up like them? They were so at ease with each other, those adults. I never had felt very much at ease with anybody.

Then one night, while a party was in full swing, I had to go to the bathroom down the hall. But the door was shut. Coming closer, I heard awful sounds. Somebody was being sick to their stomach. I waited, standing in the shadows of the hallway, for the door to open. Finally it did, and out staggered a beautiful woman in evening clothes, her face flushed, her hair wet and stringy, and a look of glazed fear in her eyes. She clung for a moment to the doorjamb, her head bowed, the acrid smell of vomit pouring out of the bathroom behind her. Then she looked up and saw me. I guess what she tried to do was smile, but what her face made was a grimace as frightening to me as a Halloween mask. Without saying anything, she lurched down the hall back to the party.

The image of that sick and frightened woman still reverberates in my mind every time I hear reference to "the Roaring Twenties." She was like a ghost in the life I led, which, however lonely, was incredibly secure.

On Saturdays my father took me out to a baseball diamond just north of the Big Stone Castle that I imagined was the home of a great dragon. But my father wasn't interested in dragons; he was interested in teaching me how to throw a ball. He brought along a softball. He'd stand some distance away and gently toss it to me. I must have been about six at the time. The ball would bump my knee, or go between my legs, or go over my shoulder. But somehow I never could connect my hands well with it. So I'd go chase it and try to throw it back. The ball would go a couple of yards to the right of him. The next one a couple of yards to the left of him. Finally I'd get mad and, with a tremendous effort, throw it ten feet over his head and right into the bushes behind him. At this point my father would sigh. Somehow I just wasn't the son he'd imagined.

And I knew it.

Try as I would to please him out there on the playing fields, some perverse awkwardness in my body led me to get tangled up, or stumble, or miss, or get preoccupied with dragons. I would want all the more to retire into my world of books and leave the playing fields to my father and all those other people who knew what to do with their bodies. I was convinced they had a special gift that God had denied me.

Something was going very wrong. I sensed it. There was a curious frightened look on my mother's face. My father was gloomy and watchful. My father would read the *Herald Tribune* at breakfast and then, with a sudden gesture, throw it on the floor. It was the world outside, I thought. Some awful things must be happening.

But the problems did not come from the outside world. My father and mother were not happy together. He was drinking heavily, neglecting his family and his work. I saw him drunk only once. He had apparently been brought home in this condition. A couple of business associates were with him and drove him for hours in an open convertible over country dirt roads, trying to sober him up. Why I was taken along for the ride, I have no idea. It was probably just a part of all the confusion. I suppose that in many, many ways I was overly protected as a child, a rich kid. Yet there is the complementary irony that I was not protected at all.

Then, one Saturday morning, crisp but sunny in late November, my father was sitting in his favorite chair in front of the Atwater-Kent, a cup of coffee in hand. I climbed into his lap. "C'mon, let's go to the park," I said.

He shook his head and sipped his coffee.

"I'll throw the ball straight. I promise."

He looked at me, his eyes tired, and tousled my hair. "I'm sure you will. Someday."

"C'mon."

"No. Not now."

I snuggled close to him and rested my head on his shoulder. I hoped his arms would hold me. But they rested on the arms of his chair. All that moved was his hand, bringing the cup to his lips.

Christmas

Several days before the Big Day, my father came home from work at lunchtime, which was strange. He never did that. After lunch was served, he announced that he was taking me on a bus ride. The day was dark, and it was snowing lightly. We climbed aboard a double-decker Fifth Avenue bus. We made it to the front seat on the top deck, which, for me, was the most exciting place in the world to be.

As the bus lumbered down the avenue past all the shops and stores gleaming with Christmas decorations, I was dazzled, but my father seemed withdrawn, and his smile was wan.

After we passed Thirty-fourth Street, with most of the big stores behind us, and headed down for the big Christmas tree in Washington Square, my father started talking about his boyhood Christmases. He told me about how his family decorated their Christmas tree with strings of berries and popcorn, lit it with candles, and kept a big pail of water beside the tree in case any of the candles tipped. He told me how they sang carols, took sled rides, and gave each other some handmade presents.

It all sounded very strange to me. The presents I expected would come gift-wrapped from F.A.O. Schwartz. Nobody

I knew ever handmade anything. And our Christmas tree decorations glimmered silver and gold. But the Fifth Avenue bus, pushing through the snowy winds . . . yes, that was kind of like a sled ride. I felt a twinge of excitement.

Still, I wondered why my father was talking to me the way he was. He'd never done that before. It was as if he were giving me presents out of his memory, handmade gifts of his past for me to keep as my very own. I was uneasy; he was so solemn about it.

On Christmas Eve, nothing so simple as sugar plums were dancing in my head, but neatly wrapped packages with big red bows. An Erector set. A chemistry set. Books by Howard Pyle. An atlas, with faraway places in bright colors. I tucked myself into bed, pulled the blankets over my head, and prayed for sleep to come and time to pass.

I heard the Christmas carols coming from the radio in the living room and, above the music, my parents' voices. I felt warm and peaceful.

The next thing I knew it was daybreak. Stillness filled the house. I climbed out of bed and walked to the window. Outside, snow fell softly. Quickly I ran into the living room. Santa Claus had already been there bringing gifts, which lay strewn about the tree.

I sneaked a look at the labels. The big square one wrapped in red tissue—that was "To Malcolm from Daddy." I really and truly wondered what that one was! I picked it up. It was heavy. The flat one with light blue tissue and a dark blue bow—that was "To Malcolm from Mother." Was that a chemistry set or an Erector set? Or maybe it was just some clothes. Ugh! I tried to figure out how to open the blue one so I could get a peek. But it was wrapped so tight, I knew it would show. Besides, I had to wait for Daddy and Mother.

When they came into the room, the mood was different from that of past Christmases. All hushed, as if somebody had died or something. When we opened the presents, I tried to be extra noisy about it, shouting and laughing and carrying on, giving my father a big hug for the set of blocks, kissing my mother for the Erector set. But it didn't do any good. Both my father and mother just smiled as if they were going to cry. I guess I wanted to cry, too. But I wanted them to think that I thought everything was going to be all right.

A couple of days later, my mother took me by the hand and led me into the living room. "Malcolm, your father and I want to talk to you." My father was sitting on the couch. The Christmas tree had been taken down. Everything was like it had always been for as long as I could remember. My mother sat in a chair in front of the fireplace. I wanted to sit on the couch beside my father, but something stopped me. I sat down on the hassock, not close to either one of them. I felt like dying.

I saw them exchange looks. Then my father started to talk. His voice was this strange monotone. "Malcolm, your mother and I are going to separate."

Separate? What could that mean?

My mother broke in. "You've got to understand, Malcolm. It wasn't your father's fault. . . . "

Another exchange of looks. My mother seemed to retreat back into a sleepwalking self.

My father put his fist to his mouth. He couldn't seem to say anything more. And the scream was inside me. Daddy, hold me!

I heard my mother's voice as if she were a teacher in school, sweet and reasonable and from another planet. "Malcolm, sometimes grownups just can't find their way. Your father and I . . . we've lost each other. Things are so different now. Maybe we'll find each other again. Maybe things will get better, soon. But . . . now . . . we've failed, Malcolm. Everything's failed. We're grownups and . . . and . . . " I saw the tension around her lips, the sag of her cheeks. I looked at my father and saw an old man. "We've failed."

My father. A sudden passion. "I'm sorry, son."

A silence.

My father's voice had an infinite tiredness. "Malcolm. Your mother and I both love you. We both want you to be safe and happy and secure."

I sat there on the hassock, trembling on the verge of nowhere.

Another silence.

I never heard my mother's voice more even, more controlled. "What we need to know, Malcolm, is whether you'd rather stay with me or go with your father. It's not going to be easy, either way. I'm going to have to move into a small apartment, and I'm going to try to find a job. Your father will have his own place."

Another silence. I looked from one to the other and hoped I was just having a bad dream. But I knew I wasn't. This was happening.

I didn't say anything. I had no idea which one I wanted to be with. I wanted to stay with both of them. I looked at my father's face, impassive there on the couch, so worn and somber.

What would I do? Where would I go? I was afraid. Things were going on all around me that I didn't understand, and

Daddy and Mother were a part of those things; however, just as I was, they also were hurt by them, angered by them. And I knew there wasn't anything I could do about those things. I had a vision of racing down strange city streets, yelling, "Daddy, help me, the monster's after me," and knowing that Daddy couldn't.

But *why?* Why did things have to be like this?

I shriveled inside. I didn't know. And how could I ask them to explain? And how could I make them stop? I felt helpless. I was desperately afraid of the plight in which I found the persons who meant more to me than anyone else in the world—that archetypal man against whom all other men in my life would be measured; that archetypal woman who had given me birth and would soon provide my home and sole source of familial love.

Ever afterward, I could not trust happiness, even when it surprised me by popping into my life much like an unexpected sunrise on an icy winter morning. Happiness would always make me feel sad as well as make me laugh, for I knew that it must be short-lived. I would always be damned grateful for crumbs. A table magnificently spread with the goodness of life would never cease to overwhelm me, but I could make no plans for a tomorrow of the same. I had learned all too well how quickly a scene in life changes. The actors depart. Costumes and props are stored away. One stands alone with ghosts inside an empty theater.

For years afterward my father's absence was a void in my life, and that void was particularly haunting around Christmastime. His Christmas present could invariably be counted on to send me into a rage that would last unabated for days.

He undoubtedly meant well. It was just that my expectations of a gift, and the emotional need wrapped up in those expectations, could not have been met by a factory of Santa Clauses working overtime. A box sent me by my father would arrive in the mail shortly before Christmas. It contained a suit I would never wear this side of death, a book I would not be interested even in perusing (yet I was an avid reader of three or four books each week), a shirt that seemed to have come out of a fire sale, and a necktie that I loathed. I threw the contents of the box on the floor. I wept. I wrote letters to my father, alternately thanking and excoriating him, and tore them up. What I needed were his arms around me. What I bitterly yearned for was his love. I could not see the expression of it that was surely contained in the box of gifts he had painstakingly prepared for his distant young son and mailed to him.

An Adirondack Vacation

One summer, when I was about ten, my mother and I spent several weeks at a big resort hotel in the Adirondack Mountains in northern New York State. Several Rockefellers, an enchanting clairvoyant from Paris, and the Episcopal bishop of New York were also staying there.

Up there in the Adirondacks was my first time among mountains. Later in Colorado and California I would see peaks far higher, crags and canyons more dramatic, but Mount Marcy—a mere five thousand feet—holds a mystery for me, a sense of wonder in its mass and presence that stays with me still. I wondered what it looked like, snowcapped in winter. Was it like Mount Olympus? Did strange Indian gods live up there? Would they descend, like Zeus and Aphrodite, Ares and Hermes, to mix their divinity with mere humans? Looking at Mount Marcy, I felt even less than mere human. I'd retreat into the nearby forests to find my scale.

My favorite place was a flat rock beside a stream. I was reading Howard Pyle's *Robin Hood* that summer, and all around me was Sherwood Forest. I'd leave the hotel after breakfast, clutching my book, and wend my way along the crunching forest floor and between the overhanging trees till I came to the flat rock and the Merry Band. I could imagine, just up the stream, that bridge where Friar Tuck established the primacy of churchly virility.

But mostly who I waited for was Will Scarlet, sauntering through the woods, sniffing on a rose. I felt a surge of excitement just reading about him and seeing Pyle's etching of him, princely and fastidious in hose and doublet—the power and mold of the legs, the bulge in the groin, chastely hidden—almost—by the doublet. I'd stroke my own puny bulge as my eyes stroked the illustration. Then I'd look up, searching through the tree trunks, hoping to catch a glimpse of him.

I had these fantasies that he'd come—and heart-stopping imaginings of what would happen if he came through the forest, noticed me, walked to the flat rock, and sat down beside me. I could see the tilt of the eyebrow, hear the lilt of the voice: "Would ye like to smell my rose?"

But Will Scarlet did not come.

Instead, one afternoon, sitting with my back propped against the rock, reading, I heard a rustle in the underbrush. Turning, I saw three boys in their early teens standing there watching me. I recognized one of them as a guest at the hotel. The other two were strangers. Something about the way the three of them looked at me, the fixity of their eyes, made me suddenly fearful. I got to my feet.

They walked down the embankment and stepped up on the flat rock while I stood on the ground. They were bigger than I was, and their standing on the rock made them bigger still. My eyes were on a level with their crotches, and the fear I felt was mingled with excitement. I didn't know what was going to happen, but secretly I wanted something strange and wonderful and gentle to happen. Maybe they'd take me away with them, camping, high in the mountains, away from everybody, and . . .

"Hi, kid." The boy had red, curly hair and a deep voice, and he wore tight shorts. "Whatcha doin'?"

"Reading," I said.

The redhead exchanged impassive glances with his two companions. "Readin', huh? Watcha waitin' for?"

"I'm not waiting for anything. I'm just sitting here reading."

The redhead arched his eyebrows in mock surprise. "You weren't waitin' for nothin'? Aw, c'mon! You knew we was comin', didn't yuh?"

"No! I was just . . . sitting here . . . reading."

"'Magine that. Just reading." He shook his head; then, with a bright grin: "Was you playin' with yourself while you read?"

"No." I felt a flush of guilt. "I wasn't playing with myself."

The redhead's hand dropped to his crotch, just a few feet away from my face. The hand had big freckles on it. "I bet you got a cute little pecker, huh?"

I stepped backward as I saw the redhead's two companions tense.

"An' how 'bout those little squirrel's nuts you're hidin' in them pants of yours?"

One of the boys, dark-haired and stocky, stepped off the rock and came close to me. The redhead slowly rubbed his crotch, his eyes on mine. "You're gonna show us that cute little pecker and them squirrel's nuts, ain't yuh?"

I shook my head, violently.

"Aw, sure you are! You're gonna drop them pants and wiggle that little thing . . . " He leered at the other two boys. "And then you're gonna bend over, yuh hear?" There was a commanding edge to his voice. "Are you a sissy or a real man? We're real men!"

The other boy, blond and lanky, the one I recognized from the hotel, now stepped down off the rock on the other side of me. I glanced at him in panic. He was from the hotel. We had something in common. Maybe he'd help. But his eyes were narrow-slitted and impassive. He grabbed my arm; his voice was barely above a whisper. "You heard what he said, didn't you?"

I felt the stocky boy's hand on my belt buckle.

There was a screaming inside my head. I wrenched away from their hands and lurched toward the stream. I knew that stream. I knew, rock by rock, how to jump across its width. But the boys didn't.

They chased me as I bounded across the water from one slippery rock to the next. First the blond boy slipped and fell into the water, crying as he twisted his leg. I didn't wait to find out what happened to the redhead, but when I reached the roadway on the other side of the stream, I was alone, panting and terrified.

I ran all the way back to the hotel.

That night I cried myself to sleep. Why had the boys done that? Why had they scared me so? Why hadn't they just taken me camping with them, high in the mountains? I'd have done anything just to be with them.

The next evening at dinner, I caught sight of the blond boy at the other end of the hotel dining room. He was limping as he walked to his table. He saw me and turned his head away quickly. I sat at our table with my mother beside me and ate my fruit cup, and I wondered what *his* pecker looked like. But I never found out. Two days later he and his family finished their vacation at the hotel and left.

The incident by the stream left haunting echoes inside my head. It was so easy to drift along, cared for by my mother, warmed by other guests' attentions, peaceful in the ordered world of the hotel, the mountains there but distant, the fantasies of Sherwood Forest seen only through a scrim of imagination. So easy. So safe. So reassuring.

But the boys, on that flat rock, they were *real!*

Barely touching my body, they had raped my psyche, thrusting their presence into vitals of mine that both yearned for them and repelled their claims. Fearing them, I feared myself. Hoping for them, I feared myself even more. Who was I, anyway? What was happening to me? And why should it happen just to me?

I could look around the hotel dining room. The husbands. The wives. The grandparents. The children. The wealthy widows and maiden aunts. Even the resplendent bishop. All so properly dressed. All so genteel in their converse and gesture. All so related by blood or marriage. All held together by social sanction and the politesse of a culture that I could later recognize as lingering colonial Victorian. Everybody had a place in it but me. How could I hide what I was? But was I? What was I? The blond kid, who was he? Did he know who he was? Yes, he had been right there in that dining room. With everybody else. Genteel. Related. Did his parents know how his eyes had slitted when he had grabbed my arm? What would he have done when they dropped my pants? I could feel the rape of him . . . that nice . . . well-bred . . . angelic . . . young man.

Who else?

I stared about the dining room in a kind of panic. No, it couldn't be! It was just us two. That was all. No one else.

This particular evening my mother and I dined as usual at the select table of the hotel manager. The manager's exit from the dining room after dinner was majestic. My mother to his right, me to his left with his protective arm around my shoulder, he would stalk the length of the dining room with lordly aplomb, pausing to speak to friends and to admiring wealthy widows. I felt myself a page boy in the royal progress and basked in its glory.

We would proceed to the veranda. The manager would enthrone himself in one of the rockers to admire the play of evening light on the crests and shoulders of the mountains. For him it was an evident aesthetic experience, to be savored as he savored good vintage wine or a deep breath of morning air. For me, remembering the terror and desire I'd felt for those three boys by the stream, it was a far darker experience. The loom of the mountains was foreboding. I could imagine Indian gods up there, staring down at me and frowning, then looking at the divining bones at their feet, signs of the years ahead for me, and shaking their heads in pity. It was as if I had a mark on my forehead that only they could see, and only they knew its meaning. Would that mark stay with me all my life? Or would it heal or fade? I felt they knew, reading the bones. But they were distant and silent.

Those were the times when I sat on the manager's lap and hoped that he, or some other gentle man, would always be there to protect me. Not even a glowering Indian god, I was sure, could prevail against such masculine dignity and strength.

Strange how all foreboding vanished when I first caught sight of Jamie checking into the hotel with his mother and father. The desire I felt for him was sudden and electric. Maybe it was those eyes, big and watchful and direct, that answered my look at him and held steady for a long moment. I wanted to go over to him right then, but there was such a bustle of clerks and bellhops and luggage that I held back. But I knew I'd know him, and I wondered how long he would be staying at the hotel.

I watched him cross the lobby to the elevator. He was about my age, but slightly built, and he walked with a spring to his step. His hair was dark, and he wore it somewhat longer than people did in those days. I wanted to tousle it. Just before he got onto the elevator, he looked at me again with a hesitant smile, and I smiled back.

At dinner that evening I watched for him in the dining room. By the time we were halfway through the main course, I was beginning to panic. He hadn't appeared. My eyes kept prowling the dining room, checking one familiar face after another. Why didn't he come? Maybe he was sick or something. Maybe they had gone someplace else to have dinner. Maybe . . . Maybe . . .

The waitress was clearing the main course at our table when Jamie and his mother and father came into the dining room and were directed to a table just two tables away from ours. I saw Jamie maneuver himself so that he could see me out of the corner of his eye.

I ate my dessert slowly and peacefully. Things, I felt, were going to be all right.

That night after dinner, I skipped being page boy to the hotel manager's royal progress to the veranda and ghosted around the lobby, listening to someone play the grand piano. The next thing I knew, Jamie was standing beside me, his eyes intent on the keyboard, his shoulder brushing, ever so lightly, against mine. I felt a lightheaded rush of excitement, my mouth went dry, and I couldn't think of anything to say. But in a few minutes, Jamie shifted on his feet. His voice was low and close to my ear. "C'mon, let's go down to the playground."

"Sure," I said, and we looked each other full in the eye.

It wasn't much of a playground. Just a slide, some swings, and a jungle gym. But we clambered up to the top of the jungle gym, sat there under the panoply of the evening sky, and talked about things, just like we'd been friends for years.

For the next week Jamie and I were inseparable. We went hiking in the woods and discovered caves. We swam in the hotel's outdoor swimming pool. We went fishing where the stream became a deep pool in a forested area just behind the hotel.

All the while, I was acutely conscious of Jamie's body. The wiry tension of his muscles. The bony structure of his face. At the same time, his cherubic lips and the gentle fleshiness of his buttocks. As we changed in the dressing room by the swimming pool, I glanced very quickly to find out what his genitals looked like, but his back was turned to me as he slipped on his trunks. Still I knew I'd find out, somehow.

At the end of the week, it happened. It was a warm day, and in the late afternoon we decided to go fishing at the stream, promising our parents we'd be home before supper. We got out our rods, lines, and hooks and settled down by an

overhanging embankment by the pool to wait for a Big
One. We waited and waited, but the Big One was not hungry. Not even the little ones were hungry. Overhead, the
trees seemed heavy in the heat, and the silence surrounded
us like a cloak. I felt us inexpressibly isolated as if Jamie and
I were the only two people in the world. We could share
whispered secrets, and no one would know. I wanted to
tell him. . . . What did I want to tell him? I wanted to touch
him. . . . Why did I want to touch him? And I didn't dare
think of where I would touch him or what would happen
if I did. Yet he was sitting there, just inches away from me!

Jamie stirred and pulled up his line. "There aren't any
fish in the pool today. C'mon, let's take a swim."

"At the hotel?"

"No. Right here. It's deep enough."

"It's getting late."

"We got time."

I felt my pulse quicken. "We don't have trunks."

"Who needs trunks? There's nobody around." And he
looked at me with those big eyes. Panic surged in me. The
secret? Did he know? Could he tell? Would it show?

I tried to sound reluctant. "Okay. If you want."

His voice was soft. "C'mon, let's do it."

I remember the fright I felt when there was no more to
take off but my underpants, the strange sense of relief when
I stood naked by the shadowed pool, the throat-tighten-
ing excitement of seeing Jamie's slight lithe body, as naked
as mine.

We tucked our clothes under the embankment. Then,
with a whoop, Jamie dived into the pool. I stood at the
pool's edge, watched Jamie's body squirming beneath the
water's surface, and felt my penis begin to harden.

Jamie broke surface with a splash and looked at me. A quick grin crossed his face. "Dive in! It's great!"

I glanced down and saw that my cock was fully erected. I began to swim. The chill of the water mercifully shriveled me. But he'd seen me; I knew that. Was that why he'd grinned? And what was he thinking when he grinned? Or was he just enjoying the swim?

We swam around for a while. Jamie would do surface dives in the deep parts of the pool, his buttocks rearing above the water as he plunged down and then disappearing beneath the shimmer. I'd never know where he was going to come up. Once I felt a light touch on my leg and he came up right beside me, laughing in a burst of spume.

The chill of the water was beginning to get to me. I got out of the water and sat on a little patch of sand by the embankment.

"What's the matter?" Jamie asked.

"I'm cold."

Jamie swam over to where I was sitting and started out of the water. But he stumbled on a rock and fell sprawling across my knees. He looked up at me, his eyes mischievous. "C'mon, we'll wrestle. That'll warm you up." He grabbed me around the neck and pushed me back on the sand. The warmth of his body sent chills through mine. I struggled (although not very convincingly, I'm afraid) against his grip as we rolled on the sand, and I finally pinioned him on his back, astride him, my hands holding his arms.

He looked up at me. "Uncle," he whispered.

I released his arms. They glided around my neck, pulling my head down to his. I stretched full length on top of him, our heads touching. Our heavy breathing from the struggle gradually subsided. I felt my penis grow hard against his body, and, pressed against mine, I felt his grow hard, too. I raised my head and looked at his face. He was looking at me. After a long moment I lowered my head till our lips touched. And held.

Then I moved over on my side next to him, and my hand reached down, slowly, until I touched the flesh of his cock. It stiffened still more, and Jamie's hips stirred. I felt a wonder. I had caused this to happen in someone else. Someone else felt as I did. I wasn't alone. There was Jamie. And now we had *our* secret.

We shared the wonder of that secret, touching, exploring, responding, till we heard voices—adult voices—calling our names. We clutched each other, then scrambled to the hiding place of the overhanging embankment and lay absolutely still, pressed against each other, our heartbeats racing.

The voices passed into the distance.

"I guess it's late," I said. "We better get dressed."

"Yeah. I guess so."

We drew apart. We dressed in silence, not looking at each other, gathered up our fishing gear, and trudged back to the hotel. We didn't say much of anything to each other. All I could think of were those voices, the voices that had wrenched us apart as surely as those adult hands might have done. What we had done was wrong—to them—and if they ever found out . . . ?

I glanced at Jamie, staring straight ahead as we walked. Would he tell? What if his parents made him tell or tricked him into admitting what we had done? Would his mother tell my mother? And would one of them tell the hotel manager?

Suddenly that slender body walking shoulder to shoulder beside me was an ominous, dangerous thing.

As we walked up the steps of the hotel, I saw Jamie look at me, and there was fear in his eyes. "You're not going to tell, are you?"

I shook my head violently.

"I won't either," he said.

But we never hung around with each other much after that. When my mother and I left the hotel to go back to the city three days later, I said good-bye to Jamie. We shook hands, solemnly, and said we hoped we'd see each other again. But we both knew we never would. Our lost playful innocence was a grim specter of the complexity of the adult world that awaited us. How did we know even then as two small boys that it was considered very, very wrong to show natural affection to one another? If we had been discovered playing a war game, it would likely have been accepted with approval.

Early School Years

The experience with Jamie is still vivid in my memory not just because it was one of the few sexual experiences of my childhood but also because it was one of the few times in those early years that I felt genuinely close to another boy. Yet male beauty left me shaken and breathless. I merely glanced at it, learned how to absorb its total eroticism in what appeared to be a casual turn of my eyes, and quickly looked away. Occasionally when I stood transfixed in sheer hunger and wonder before a godlike male apparition of utter beauty, my face burned in recognition that I had revealed what must remain a secret about my deepest feelings.

There were unmistakable implications of male same-sex love that leapt out of pages of books into my consciousness. When I was a youngster, David and Jonathan in the Bible could almost make me cry, because I yearned to share myself like that with another boy. Oh, to die for one's young male lover, a boy with shining, explosive dark eyes and a lithe body one held nakedly in a warm embrace of understanding and love.

At school I studied arithmetic, geography, *Silas Marner,* international relations, Latin, and biology. Out of all that education, couldn't someone have taught me about the place of gay experience in the history of the human race? I was given no gay role models. A few naturally dawned on me. Looking at Michelangelo's depiction of God's creation of man and seeing the unabashedly physical and lusty man who served as the model, I grasped a deep truth that stayed with me. Michelangelo was, I knew, a brother.

One thing that I was taught in school was priorities. Success, recognition, and making money must always come first in a balanced life. This is no doubt why dozens of people whom I know make their life decisions—love, marriage or union, where they live, what kind of work they do—on the basis of money instead of their real needs and yearnings. But life is so short.

Thoreau said that a person who does not keep pace with companions perhaps hears a different drummer. Keep step to the music that you hear, however measured or far away, he urged. Society does not want people to listen to different drummers. It establishes common fantasies to be shared by all. These are fantasies concerning women, men, blacks, gays, success, failure, sexuality, death, and life. But even in high school I heard a different drummer. However, I could not keep step to the music that I heard. I stumbled and fell. I felt that I was torn apart.

The idea of two men making love, or two women embracing and coming to a climax, was too different from everything I was taught for me to cope with it. Wasn't it terribly wrong? A sin against God and nature? Debauchery and decadence?

By the time I reached adolescence, I was a frail youngster who read a lot of books, extraordinarily intense and solitary. My intermittent friendships with a few other boys usually ended abruptly and without explanation. I believed that the fault lay within me, a result of what I assumed to be my personal ineptness in sustaining relationships. For the most part I looked at the outside world of boys my own age like a prisoner looking through a barred cell window. I felt locked in the cell of myself, and I ached to get out.

I felt at that time in my life a particular attachment to but also fear of men and masculinity. On one occasion I visited in a house where I saw two men, wearing only their shorts, seated in a bedroom. Their easy camaraderie, with a sense of male secrets shared and easy body contact between them, made me feel like an outsider. Had I missed an initiation into maleness? If I had been with them in that room, I would have remained rigid and aloof. The full impact of what I understood to be maleness was ambiguous and confusing.

In the place of hard, violent energy I preferred grace, warmth, and gentleness. I hated feeling forced to play any kind of a prescribed role. I was developing as a highly individual young human being who disliked conformity as a necessary part of life.

Most adults were, in my opinion, obviously playing a game of lies with me. "Hello, Malcolm," they said. They smiled and were jovial. But they knew, as well as I did, that they were a million miles away from where I was. My best defense was to give the impression that they were communicating with me. I deliberately failed to do this once when the solicitous wife of a Protestant minister condescendingly asked me at a tea party what book I was reading.

"*The Life of Catherine de' Medici,*" I replied.

"My, my," she said. "Is that the best reading for a sweet little boy like you? What movies do you like to see, dear?"

"*The Scarlet Empress* with Dietrich is my favorite," I replied.

She smiled vaguely, took another cookie to eat with her cup of tea, and drifted away.

During junior high school, I was excused from gym classes at the behest of a physician who felt that I had a slight heart condition. No such problem ever showed up later in my life, but his decision removed me from a natural environment with my own sex that I needed very much. For years afterward I knew a constraint with males in place of naturalness and ease.

On a visit to the New York World's Fair in 1939 I became cruelly aware of the fact that I could not urinate in the immediate presence of another boy or man. I walked into a public restroom and waited in line at a urinal, but when my turn came to stand before it I could not function. This condition (which I later learned many other men share) persisted for years. Only when I became comfortable and relaxed in the presence of other men did the problem disappear.

Inevitably, such childhood experiences introduced sexual inhibitions. The cumulative effect created estrangement from my male peers, evidenced by numerous scenes from my school years.

Loneliness and Companionship

High school in Denver was a complex time for me. I attended a snobbish, posh school with a closed caste system. Saturday mornings I walked to the public library to leave a stack of books and check out new ones. One morning, as I approached the library with my books, I encountered two classmates, both football players. One was the president of my class. To them I was apparently a misfit, an intellectual queer who was bookish and withdrawn. Without saying a word, but as if it had been planned, both boys suddenly placed their hands beneath my bottom and crotch, lifted me into the air, spilled my books on the ground, and then walked away laughing. A proud youngster, I was mortified, hurt, and enraged. Without looking around at them, almost without breaking my stride, I picked up the books with what dignity I could muster and continued walking into the library.

Still, misfit though I appeared to be, I was like other youths in my participation in the typical puberty rites of crushes, drinking with the gang, and the desire to go steady. But my idea of going steady was very different from the heterosexual norms that were exalted at the high school.

Ralph, to my eyes, was the most beautiful boy in the school, tall, dark-haired, athletic, with an easygoing grace that I found irresistible. He was everything that I was not. I was awed by his popularity and envious of his intelligence. I felt electric desire just being in the same room with him, and I daydreamed of his nakedness.

But I couldn't work up the nerve to say anything to him, not even a passing "hello." And then . . . a miracle. He said "hello" to me!

I came out of my cell of self to be with him. I vastly enjoyed the times we spent together, rowing on a park lake, walking, talking, laughing, trashing around, and wasting time gloriously. We were a strange Mutt-and-Jeff combination, but he seemed to enjoy my company and line of chatter, and I reveled in his nearness. Once he told me about a strip poker game he had played with two girls and another boy. I imagined how exciting it would be to play strip poker with just the two boys. I almost worked up my courage to suggest it, but not quite.

I thought of Jamie and the mountain pool in the Adirondacks. There would be far grander ones out here in the Rockies. . . . Would he respond as Jamie had responded?

All around us at the school, boys and girls were going steady. In my naivete and innocence, it occurred to me that that was what Ralph and I were doing, too, only we'd never said it. I wanted to say it.

One evening, out in the park, with other couples going by, hand in hand, I looked at Ralph. "That's what we're doing, too, isn't it? Going steady."

I saw his eyes flash and his face set. "You're crazy, Malcolm. Boys don't go steady with boys. If you're like that, I never want to speak to you again!"

He turned on his heel and walked away. And he never spoke to me again.

I felt an awful embarrassment and sense of betrayal. I believed I had been misunderstood cruelly. The incident caused me to become more introverted and less trusting of others. I felt that I could not take another risk like that in a human relationship. This meant I could not be open to anyone. The necessity of consciously playing a role in a long-run masquerade became a part of my awareness.

All during those years I sought relief from the tension of playing the masquerade, trying to find some way to express the affection that other boys expressed so easily and enviably with girls.

When I was a lonely youngster, my mother had given me a collie—Laddie—and I lavished affection on him, grooming his long hair that swung so regally when he walked, parading him around the neighborhood with his studded collar, dog tag, and chain, playing tag and stick-throw with him in open fields, while he responded with mischief in his eye. In the evenings he would curl up beside me while I lay on the floor reading or listening to the radio, and he would go to sleep. My hand on his chest, I could feel his heart beat sturdily, see his paws make running motions as he chased some dream rabbit. I remember my acute embarrassment when, lolling in sleep, he would get a hard-on. Was he chasing a girl dog . . . or a boy dog? I reached the sad conclusion. Natural animal that he was, he probably liked girl dogs better than me.

Still, I knew he loved me. The way his eyes would light up when I came into the room. How he would yelp and scratch at the door when I'd shut him in the house. The way he'd prance when I reached for his collar and chain. When everybody else was a million miles away, there was always Laddie, poking me with his paw or brushing against my leg.

Then one day Laddie disappeared. I searched the neighborhood, calling his name, expecting him to come bounding out from behind a bush or a parked car. I turned a corner, and there he was, lying on a street curb. Something was strange about how he lay.

"Laddie!"

No response.

I ran to him. His head was twisted. His eyes were open. And he did not move.

I felt his chest for that sturdy beat. But I could feel no movement. In a sudden, drenching moment, I was sobbing. Laddie was dead, and everyone else was a million miles away.

Strange how the episode repeated itself in a much more tragic form. During summer vacation in Colorado—it must have been about the time I was finishing high school—I had a temporary job on the maintenance crew of the parks department. I liked the outdoor work, the crispness of the air, the sight of the mountains, but I was no good at handling a paintbrush and even worse at tending plants. One of the other members of the crew was an older youth named Chad who was on summer vacation from his junior year at George Washington University in St. Louis. Chad and I worked together on the crew and became friends.

I needed that friendship, and I wanted it to grow. Here was one person, I thought, whom I might be able to trust with my confusions, my aches, and my loneliness. I had no reason to believe he was gay; he had a girlfriend down in Pueblo whom he saw regularly. But he had steady, thoughtful eyes, and there was a gentleness about him that showed up vividly as we went about the park grounds doing garden work. I watched the patience with which he would fertilize and mulch the earth around the plants, the delicacy of his pruning, the care he took in staking growing stalks. I saw in Chad's gardening a new meaning for "reverence for life."

We talked about a lot of things as we worked together. I told him stories about the people I had interviewed for the high school paper. I went on with my remembrances of what it was like to live in New York City (he'd never been to New York). He told me about camping in the Rockies and a trip he had made to New Orleans. I asked him a lot of questions about college.

But I never mentioned my father. And I never told him about how I thought he was . . . well . . . beautiful, that I thought a lot of men were beautiful and I didn't know what to do about it. No, I didn't tell him that.

I was almost sure that he wouldn't have reacted the way Ralph had reacted, just turning on his heel and walking out of my life. He would listen, with a friendly look in those thoughtful eyes, and maybe he could help me understand myself and what was going on around me, shaping and influencing my life.

Time after time, I came almost to the verge of saying, "Chad, I've got this problem. . . ." But the moment never seemed quite right. I thought, not this summer, but maybe next summer I can get up my nerve. Or even when we're both back for Christmas vacation.

Chad left to go back to college in St. Louis, driving with a couple of his classmates. Somewhere in the Ozarks they had an accident. Chad was thrown from the car and killed.

Knowing in high school that I was secretly tainted, would never be an athletic star or the most popular stud on campus, I threw myself into work for the student newspaper, interviewed artists and lecturers for it (Lotte Lehmann, Kirsten Flagstad, Marian Anderson, Jascha Heifetz, Carl Van Doren, Harold J. Laski, Wanda Landowska), was *Denver Post* correspondent from the school, won the Sons of the American Revolution essay contest, placed third in the annual poetry competition, and won honorable mention in a *Scholastic* magazine contest for youthful writers. I read *The New Republic, The Nation, Harper's,* and the *Atlantic Monthly;* listened to the Metropolitan Opera broadcasts on Saturdays; and dreamed of a bright, happy, utterly stimulating world in which I would meet the most interesting, fashionable, attractive, and brilliant people who ever lived.

Deeply religious, I spent Sundays in church, but knew that the prophetic Jesus whom they talked about all the time wouldn't be allowed three feet up the center aisle if he happened to pay a visit.

In spite of the nebulous awareness of sexual feelings I have described so far, I did not really develop on a sexual plane until later in life. Therefore, sexuality did not come to front and center for me in high school. I dated girls occasionally, but the dates were sexless. We went dancing and always double- or triple-dated. The evenings would end with a late snack at Murphy's. Seated six, eight, ten, or twelve at an immense table, we regaled each other with funny stories as we ate hamburgers, potato salad, and dill pickles. We had fun. One reason was that it seemed wicked to stay out so late.

I was one of four close male friends who ran together. At times we *really* had fun—the three other boys and I—when we climbed a forbidden stone wall to visit a purportedly haunted house on a cold moonlit night, or stuck chewing gum on the doorbells of hapless victims on Halloween, or got drunk when the family of a boy had gone away on a trip and we had the whole house to ourselves. Two of the four died as young men. One was killed in World War II; the other shot himself.

Once when the four of us were at a drive-in, somebody pointed out several truck drivers walking out of a parking-lot men's room. They rubbed their crotches and laughed. A captive "queer" inside had "gone down" on them, we were made to understand. So, I thought, *that* was homosexuality. Surely, no connection between that and me could be possible. It would take a devastatingly long time before a concept of gay life as something furtive and melancholy would change for me into healthy, life-giving realities.

My gay sexuality remained submerged, by what power of the will I can now only wonder at, during this period of my maximum sexual intensity.

One incident laden with sexual connotations remains as fresh in my mind as if it had happened yesterday. It was in 1943. The United States was at war. I was riding a train on my way to college for the first time. Military priorities having juggled civilian travel schedules, I was stuck overnight in a lonely train terminal. A caring man invited me to share a mattress on the floor of an office in the terminal and get a good night's sleep. Blankets were provided for us. Noticing that he slept in the raw, I also stripped bare. I lay down beside him. Immediately I felt sexual arousal of a most intense nature. He asked if I would please get up and turn out the light. I did so hurriedly, hoping that he would not notice my erection. He went to sleep. I listened to him snore for a long time before I could relax and drift off to sleep. I believed that, for me, there lay ahead endless, hopeless nights without sexual fulfillment or joy. The next morning I resumed my trip to the campus.

The College Campus

In college, I dated for appearance's sake and because I liked to dance and be in the social company of others. I made obsessive efforts to achieve acceptable sexuality via the fraternity life. I joined the jock fraternity, dated a number of girls, and hung my Greek pin on two or three at successive intervals. I worked for, then deserted, the conventional and sternly controlled college newspaper and founded (was editor-publisher of) the *Bar Nuthin,* a raunchy, bitchy, widely read gossip sheet.

One summer during my college years I dated a beauty queen. What made her become interested in me? I had no money, social position, athletic prowess, or observable glamour. Perhaps in my own way I offered a certain excitement as a nonconformist. She danced like a goddess, and I loved to dance and was good at it. I had taught myself by buying a "how to dance" book, blocking out the steps, and practicing alone while listening to the music of Glenn Miller, Tommy and Jimmy Dorsey, and Claude Thornhill on the radio.

Beyond a kiss, there would be no sex play between the beautiful young woman and me. This was surely evident by the second or third date. However, we kept dating. We double-dated with another college woman and the most beautiful male youth I had ever laid eyes on. I could scarcely breathe normally when I was close to him, holding eye contact and basking in the scent of his healthy and tempting maleness. I would surely have embraced and practiced my gay sexuality at that time if he had been gay and offered me the companionship of his body and soul. However, he was not gay. We continued the heady double-dating.

Another woman I dated had the magic quality of a campus Vivien Leigh. She fascinated me. Her background included impeccable social position coupled with an irritating lack of money. This made her restless, imprisoning her in the need to engineer a lucrative marriage. A latent quality of wild abandon lurked just beneath her exterior perfect manners. She swore in a very chic way. Her jet black eyes and hair were striking. We spent a lot of time together, drinking, dancing, swimming, mostly talking.

My date with the acknowledged campus whore was a highlight of my college career. She was gorgeous. Her blond hair, magnificent body, and perfect carriage caused other girls to hate her, especially because her family background was working class, and she did nothing to disguise it. Most of the eligible campus males had dated her. Her reputation for sexual prowess was as well established as the date of the founding of the college. However, she enraged half of the establishment and amused the other half when she portrayed the Virgin Mary in a church Christmas pageant. Why did she accept my invitation for a date? God knows. My dancing did not bore her. Nor did my conversation. But she had a night off as a sex queen.

I drank a lot of beer at nights in the Speedway Club, a chic joint where the "in crowd" hung out. We joked, laughed, and horsed around a lot, assuming *these* were the days, and that their glamour, privilege, and self-indulgence would certainly continue uninterrupted after graduation. But, of course, I also lived constantly in a kind of hell, a world split down the middle between hard social contradictions and insoluble personal dilemmas.

During the fraternity initiation rituals I felt especially a stranger. I was physically attracted to the lusty young men around me, yet was unable to reveal my feelings and emotions. Pledges were stripped, paddled on the bare ass, then forced to pick up an olive seed in the rectum, or else suck a raw egg into the rectum, and hold it there while walking across a room, all the while maintaining an erection. Or, inside a room of naked brothers one masturbated in front of the rest. One form of hazing was the measurement of penises, first preceding an erection, then after a hard-on. There was a lot of goosing.

A homosexual person hiding my identity, I was compelled to play a constant role in fraternity life. One day an older brother who apparently found my behavior suspicious and had been drinking heavily shouted at me, "I'm going to take your pants down, beat the shit out of your ass, get your cock up, and see what's wrong with you." Another brother intervened, and I was saved an ordeal and a beating.

When I occasionally slept with my fraternity father in the dormitory, it was a warm and happy experience, but I did not dare let it be erotic. I also did not dare acknowledge even to myself that I wanted it to be.

One of my fraternity brothers was a young man named Chuck. He wore a crew cut, had a broad face with a pug nose, and came on like Andy Hardy, all-American as apple pie. He had a wide range of interests, an infectious enthusiasm, and a great sense of humor. We used to have lunch together quite often, and our talk would range all over the place from astronomy (he was a comet buff) to the Andrews sisters. But we never talked much about sex. I certainly wasn't going to bring the subject up and ramble on mendaciously about my triumphs with beauty queens. And Chuck? Well, he just didn't seem interested. Girls didn't seem half as wonderfully mysterious as comets. Years later, I learned that during World War II he was allegedly discovered kissing a male officer in the backseat of a military car. Shortly after he was placed under arrest, he committed suicide.

I wonder now at the bizarre self-deceit of it all. Those fraternity initiations were all very macho, and the participants would, for the most part, go on in life as firmly self-convinced straights, taking their roles in business or the professions, marrying and raising families, frightened or downright terrorized by any suggestions of deviation. Yet as a sexually mature gay, I can look back on those rites that took place in the privacy of the frat house and recognize them, under their cover of boisterous status assertion, for what they were—exercises in homosexual sadomasochism and voyeurism.

So long as the rites were contained as ceremonies of fraternity life, to be passed on from one generation to another, they were socially permissible. After all, boys will be boys. And some kind of ceremony is part of any initiation. But the blatant sexual content of these particular rites was a revealing glimpse of the latency that lurks just beneath the surface of straight society.

Hollywood

After graduating from college, I went to Hollywood, where I worked for the next eight years in advertising, film, radio, and the new field of television. I was at the crossroads that most people also face at the just-graduated stage. I had to decide between the priorities of a career and personal, sexual ones. Like the majority of people, I chose at the expense of my sexuality. My decision was based at least partly on the supposition that my sexual self was not as mature as my career self—or, alas, as important.

I never had truly good times. I drove myself too hard, simply wanting symbols of success to compensate in some measure for the growing vacuum of unhappiness and incompleteness that lay at the center of my life. I was in Babylon, attending all the parties, self-consciously enacting the role of a rising young golden boy—alone. My image of homosexuality remained distasteful beyond redemption, so I utterly repressed my sex.

During these years I moved in a world of movie stars, gossip columns, extravagant parties, lavish homes, hotel suites, VIP privileges, expense accounts, the best restaurants, Academy awards (I was a voting member of the Academy of Motion Picture Arts and Sciences), and inner insecurities.

It seemed to me that many people in Hollywood were locked into self-manufactured roles that they played humorlessly, no matter what the cost was to themselves or anyone else. Probably this is why my friendship with Mary Pickford mattered a lot to me. We met in a routine business way when I was employed by a film studio in which she owned a controlling interest.

She had been the first great woman screen star, preceding Garbo, Harlow, Crawford, Davis, Hepburn, Taylor, and Monroe. But she had long ago quit acting. A legend and a millionairess, Mary possessed imperial social power and was a world celebrity. Franklin D. Roosevelt had suggested that she run for the U.S. Senate, but she was content to keep outside the fray.

Mary, her husband, Buddy Rogers, and I formed a production firm, which we called P.R.B., Inc., from our initials. I worked very hard developing programs, but there was also ample time to get to know Mary very well.

We became friends. Ours was the most honest relationship I had in the world of Hollywood. Although when she was in public Mary locked herself in the iron mask of her long-run role as "America's sweetheart," privately she did not give a damn. She was rich as Croesus and famous as the Golden Fleece, and her career was all behind her. She enjoyed a good pillow fight as much as a drink. We relaxed and played. Mary never locked me inside any role. As much as I allowed her to, she let me be myself.

But I was not yet ready to be myself. I looked down on homosexuals; they were to be held in contempt and laughed at without mercy. I despised softness in men. Two men together were suspect in my eyes. I worked with two men who were homosexual. Once one of them telephoned me to say that his lover had walked out on him. He cried as he told me. The whole thing seemed so remote and distant from my life. Why couldn't the goddamn faggots manage their own shitty business, take defeat like men, hide their lousy tears, and at least smile in public like the court jesters and minstrels they were meant to be?

I had to admit, however, there was one gay union that I secretly envied. The two men were sophisticated as I longed to be, charming, warm, seemingly very happy, smart to a fault, and more talented than anyone else around. I wished that they would invite me to dinner. They never did.

But another man I knew fit the myriad of unhappy stereotypes of the homosexual. He was really too young to be as seedy as he was. He wore flaws like some men wear ties. His eyes expressed disappointment and failure of nerve. He came on so weakly that one wanted to slap him sharply on the back and say, "Christ, man, get on with it! Do something! Move it!" Since he was so obviously a failure, most people rejected him out of hand.

He edited a little magazine that would shortly die. No one who was anybody read it. He lived in the most broken-down hotel I had ever seen. It could have been a stage setting for Tennessee Williams's *Camino Real,* a phantasmagoria of exotic lost dreams and shifting fantasies. Indeed, the man himself could estimably have been cast as the broken priest in *Night of the Iguana.* One night I visited the hotel where he lived. We had drinks in the bar, a physical prefiguring of hell filled with lost, lonely people who were seated isolated from each other amid plastic palm trees.

The man asked me to stay. Christ, I wanted to. I was so lonely, so horny, so much in need of the tenderness that he could give. But I believed that I would lose my secure hold on my life if I opened myself up to his needs and strengths and let all my defenses and masks fall like so much rusty armor to the floor. I believed that I would never again be able to control all the intricate apparatus of my life that was exactly in place, each piece where I knew to find it. I was playing a train conductor, and my life was the train. It was awful that night to say no and walk away.

Once I spent two weeks in Mary Pickford's guest house while I was recuperating from an illness. I was up and around one rainy night toward the end of my stay when Miss Pickford was giving one of her celebrated parties. One of the guests was a distinguished film director whom I'll call Brewster. He was an imposing man, tall, ramrod straight, with close-cropped iron-gray hair and an aquiline face. He radiated authority—as directors probably should. According to Hollywood gossip, he had a taste for handsome young actors, and presumably he had no difficulty in fulfilling his taste, since getting a part in one of his films was the dream of every young actor who aspired to a career in film. If the director wanted to be served, undoubtedly he was served— handsomely.

After an exchange of glances at the party, I had put Brewster, in my narcissistic way, out of my mind. After all, I was no aspiring actor. But it was raining. And Brewster had been driven to the party by a couple who had left early. Now he was without wheels, and being without wheels in Los Angeles is like being quadriplegic anyplace else. I happened to be near him as he sat in that Versailles of moviedom—Pickfair—with a phone in his hand, trying to get a taxicab. He barked into the phone as if he were chastising an erring wardrobe mistress, but it did no good whatever. There would be no taxis available for at least an hour. Brewster put the receiver in the cradle, fuming. It was rather pathetic to see this man, who would galvanize a whole film studio, sitting there immobilized.

"I'll be glad to drive you home," I said.

He looked at me. I should have recognized that look, but I did not. All I was thinking was how to get the poor man home.

"Thank you," he said. "That's very kind of you." And his eyes roved over my figure. I felt uncomfortable, but, after all, ours was not a relationship between a powerful film mogul and someone who desired his help.

But when we got in the darkened intimacy of the car, a thought flickered through my head about just how it would be if I were an aspiring actor. The power he emanated had a vibrant sexuality. An impressionable actor might be putty in his hands.

But with me, I thought hastily, he can keep his hands to himself.

As I drove down Sunset Boulevard, he talked about the party and others he had been to at Pickfair, lacing his descriptions with charming—but poisonous—anecdotes of the human follies of the guests. We were alone together, he was entertaining me, and I was flattered. His presence, close to me in the car, seemed no longer threatening, and when I felt the light brush against my arm as he reached in his pocket for a cigarette, I did not recoil. In fact, I speculated wistfully about what happened to all those aspiring actors.

I felt his hand on my knee. I let it rest there, trying to keep it motionless as I moved my foot on the accelerator, driving down the garishly lit boulevard in the pouring rain. His talk was hypnotic, and any disturbance of its flow would have seemed offensive. Then I felt the hand move slowly, very slowly, up from my knee. I glanced at his face, close beside me, lit by the neon signs along the way—red, then green, then yellow . . . red and blue . . . red and blue . . . a flash of white, and then red and blue again.

Christmas. My father's face.

I shuddered and pulled my leg away.

The hand withdrew. There was just a slight pause in his flow of talk, and it continued. But I seemed to hear a sharper, more incisive edge to it.

As I turned off the flatlands and up into the darkened Hollywood hills where Brewster lived, he grew silent. He just sat there and emanated. I sat beside him and cringed, hoping we'd soon come to his house.

Then I felt his arm around my shoulder. There was no way I could get away from that and still drive the car. I just froze. I sensed him looking at me as if I were a butterfly on a pin, captive beauty to be cherished and plundered.

His voice was low, obscenely intimate. "The house is the white one, right there on the corner."

I slowed and stopped the car by the front walk into the house.

Brewster made no move. The voice, again: "Would you like to come in and have a drink?"

"Thanks . . . but . . . you see . . . it's just . . . " I floundered. "It's just . . . I have a hard day tomorrow . . . and I really . . . " My voice trailed off.

"You mean, you would *not* like to come in and have a drink?"

His arm was still around my shoulder. My voice must have sounded like a captive cry. "I've got to go home and get some sleep."

"You could sleep here."

"No. Listen, Brewster, all I wanted to do was to see that you got home out of the rain!"

"You led me on . . . "

"No. Honestly . . . "

"All this way . . . "

"Brewster, believe me."

"And then you chicken out, you cockteaser!" His eyes were blazing now, like coals in the darkness. "I don't like crummy little cockteasers!"

He pulled his arm from around my shoulder, opened the car door, and lunged out, slamming the door behind him. I saw him stomp up the walk to his house and let himself in. He never looked back.

I drove back to the flatlands, thoroughly unsettled—by his carnivorous need to have sex with a stranger, a just-anybody who had taken the trouble to drive him home, and by the frustration and rage that had boiled up in him when he was thwarted.

Was this the kind of life I could look forward to if I sought to fulfill my sexual needs? Would I be frantically searching from stranger to stranger to find some night's solace? Would I be trying to hypnotize some youth with displays of my aging charms just to find strength in his young flesh?

I ached for Brewster.

And I ached for myself.

The success I saw close up in Hollywood scared me to death. It seemed selfish, empty, arrogant, and quite loveless. I wanted no part of it as a permanent fixture in my life. Yet

I was apparently on a collision course with it. The unfulfilling aspects of both my career and my sexuality were bringing me to a life-acceptance crisis. How could I alter my life?

I wanted to get close to people and, I hoped, be of service to them. Yet I was hemmed in by patterns of living. Was there a chance that I could open up my life, breathe fresh air, and allow new dimensions to replace stale, closed-in spaces?

A Search for Love

CHAPTER TWO

Early in 1951 my claustrophobia in Tinseltown got the better of me. I had to escape every so often. I spent some weekends by myself in the desert. I would pack myself an overnight case and head east until I crossed the California border at the Colorado River and drove into Arizona's Yuma Desert. I took one book with me: the Bible.

At a roadside stand, I would buy a couple of bottles of chilled Coke, and then, way out in the middle of nowhere, I'd park the car by the side of the road, take my bottles of Coke and the Bible, walk out into the parched land, sit down on a rock, and read, and think. Sometimes just think. Sometimes not even that. Just let the silence wash over me.

It is strange, or maybe not so strange, that three of the world's great religions—Judaism, Christianity, and Islam—all came out of the desert. Perhaps it has to do with the immensity of sky and the sharp horizon that divides it from the earth. Unlike mothering forests, the earth in the desert is only a place to stand on; all the rest is mysterious blue infinity. It invites the human spirit to wonder.

And I wondered.

I found in the Bible not just the saccharine reassurances
I'd learned as a child. In the Psalms and the book of Lamen-
tations there were the strangest anguishes. God was not just
"my shepherd" but also "a bear lying in wait, a lion in secret places." What did that mean? I could think what it
meant to me. Had God implanted in me, in my sexuality,
a destructive beast that could destroy me? I knew my "lion
in secret places." Still . . . could I, like the Psalmist, reach
beyond my anguishes?

The sky above me was so big, so silent . . . so foreboc-
ing. Yet, in the desert, it enveloped me, gave me the air I
breathed, the sun that warmed me, the space to lift my arms
and shout reckless questions to the infinite.

Seated on my rock, I saw, a yard or so away, a Gila monster. It was a repulsive-looking reptile, as poisonous as I felt
myself. I looked at it. It looked at me and continued on its
way across the scruffy desert land. It was, to all appearances,
quite unconcerned about its looks or nature. I wondered
about that, too. If God, for his mysterious purposes, could
make a Gila monster, did God not also, perhaps, have a
purpose for me?

Emotional Starvation

In the fall of 1951 I entered divinity school in Berkeley, California, to begin my studies for the Episcopal priesthood. The stories of my peers among the gay seminarians complemented my own personal experience. The homosexual presence in the seminary was necessarily secretive, expressed by innuendo, and was found in the nighttime world of students. One gay senior, immediately after his graduation, talked to me in his room. Sweat poured off his face. He spoke of the struggle to be himself in the midst of a long, arduous experience that had seemingly been designed to change him into a desired ecclesiastical image. Another gay seminarian later married; yet another had a bout with drinking and subsequently regained his physical and spiritual health.

Most of us drank too much on occasion as a way of releasing all the pressures of seminary, including our own private ones as closeted homosexuals. I was totally closeted and did not have a single sexual experience with anyone else in the seminary, despite lush gossip to the contrary. Years later a fellow seminarian, now a priest, told me that he had been in love with me at that time. This fact, coupled with our being together because we enjoyed one another's company, led to the gossip. Inevitably, my having come from H-o-l-l-y-w-o-o-d to the seminary added combustible fuel to the sacred flames.

At that time I had nothing to confess about homosexuality except that I "had" it. I enjoyed no sex life. I got through the first three years of seminary life with only sporadic, unsatisfactory, and guilt-ridden self-sex. I prayed, "Lord, I am unworthy. Purify me. *Burn me. Burn* away the dross."

While in seminary I suffered from attacks of colitis over an extended period of time and had to go on a diet of baby foods. A hospital examination, involving a week's stay and numerous internal X rays, indicated that nothing physical was wrong. Meanwhile, the role model for a young clergyman (clergywomen were virtually nonexistent then) was a man of the cloth married to an ideal mate in a conventional, nuclear-family setting. It is not surprising that every so often our inner tensions erupted. We wreaked minor havoc on seminary property by engaging in after-hours water fights or else marched up neighboring streets late at night attired in drapes and swinging incense pots.

We were so damned lonely, caught up in the ultimately impersonal machinery of an ecclesiastical factory. Although I enjoyed the companionship of other seminarians, I thought sometimes that I would die of a stark aloneness that cut so deep because it could not be shared. A certain pattern of behavior was expected of all of us—conformist, middle-class, family-oriented, and always subject to the snap of a finger of an authority figure. Yet I believed that Christianity directly addresses the individual, the nonconformist, and the person who stands in critical opposition to established and powerful authority.

My loneliness was at times intolerable. God came to me in the white wafer that a priest administered at the communion rail of the seminary chapel, but I lay suffering alone in bed night after night. I could not share with anyone the agonies and passions, the joys and appetites of my human nature. I hated myself. I hated myself as a closeted homosexual. Why had God visited this leprosy upon me? Why had I been born? Wasn't this too much of a cross to bear forever? After all, Jesus was on his cross for approximately three hours, at least in liturgical tradition, and he died for the sins of the world. Thirty years of hanging on a cross simply as social punishment for my God-given nature began to seem excessive punishment of a distinctly cruel and unusual nature.

Years later, I was able to identify my feelings at that time with these words of Tennessee Williams in his *Memoirs:* "My greatest affliction, which is perhaps the major theme of my writings, the affliction of loneliness that follows me like a shadow, a very ponderous shadow too heavy to drag after me all the days and nights."

My loneliness was, of course, partly of my own making. I was terrified of emotional nakedness with people I knew and would continue to know—classmates and faculty members at the seminary. But that doesn't account for an incident that happened when I went to Baja California for a two weeks' outing alone.

I ended up at a small town on the Mexican coast—pleasant and quiet with a good beach and a lot of Mexican families who minded their own business. Not a clergyman in sight! I lay on the beach, soaked up the sun, and read detective stories or watched the ocean waves.

One afternoon, basking on the beach, I sensed a rush of energy nearby and watched a youthful male figure run full speed into the water, go into a flat-out racing dive, swim a hundred yards out into the Pacific at full tilt, turn and swim the distance back to shore, and emerge from the water with as much energy as he had entered it, shaking the water out of his hair.

Jeremy was from Cleveland, a sophomore at Western Reserve, who had spent the earlier part of summer bumming around Europe exploring Roman ruins. "Ever since Rome fell and the Christians took over, it's been downhill all the way," he observed.

I did not tell him that I was studying for the priesthood. After two years of seminary, his apostasy seemed quite refreshing—and he himself boyishly beautiful.

We sat on the beach and talked. He told me where he had been in Europe. Switzerland. "A lot of cows in Switzerland," he said. "With me, it's just been one goddamn amphitheatrum after another." He had a happy grin on his face. "And the Colosseum . . . holy mackerel! That's the biggest place in the whole world! And all the things that must have gone on there. Gladiators and all that. And Christians being eaten. Huh. When it comes to Christians, I'm on the side of the lions."

I was curious. "What makes you so down on Christians?"

He looked at me directly, his face worthy of Michelangelo, his eyes intent. "They give people like me a hard time."

This youth from Cleveland, he could have been an acolyte! "What do you mean—people like you?"

He stared out over the ocean. "That's the great thing about traveling around, you know? I meet you. You meet me. All the hell-and-gone in Mexico. We'll never see each other again. I can tell you things I couldn't ever tell anybody back in Cleveland."

What was I getting into, a pastoral counseling situation? Then I had a flash thought, and I hoped my pulse didn't show on the side of my neck. I tried to make my voice sound appropriately pastoral—clinical but sympathetic. "What would you like to tell me?"

He looked at me again from under his brow, his eyes watchful and just a bit seductive. "I'm queer. I like men. I'm a faggot. Christians like to burn up people like me."

I was silent for a long moment.

"What's the matter?" Jeremy said. "Aren't you gonna scream at me or run away or something? I might be contagious."

All I wanted to do was take him in my arms. I wanted to take him back to my hotel and make love to him, letting all my emotion flow over him. Who would know—in Cleveland or Berkeley? Who would care in the warm Mexican sun? All I had to do was reach out a hand to him. . . .

But I couldn't. Not even to a stranger hundreds of miles away from home. All I could do was be pastoral to a poor unfortunate. For such an act of condescending Christian charity, I felt I rather deserved to be eaten by a lion.

Jeremy moved on the next day for guacamole-cum-margaritas in Acapulco, leaving me with a plethora of garish fantasies about what might have happened in Baja California.

Back in Berkeley, as hung-up, lonely—and virginal—as ever, I went on a monastic retreat at a house high in the Sierra Nevada. One of those attending the retreat was a devout Episcopal layman whom I will call Jonathan Frazier. He was an investment banker with offices on Montgomery Street in San Francisco and a large house in the Berkeley hills, where he lived with his wife and two children. He was a financial adviser to the diocese and on the board of trustees of various Episcopal agencies in the Bay Area.

The word around the seminary was "watch out for Jonathan!"

I had a fair idea what there was about Jonathan to watch out for. The problem was that I found him very attractive and so watched out for him in not quite the way the warning was intended. In stark, and very private, reality, I wanted to go to bed with him.

He was in his early forties. He had an ascetic face, right out of a cathedral niche, a lanky body, and an impeccable wardrobe, and he drank—prodigiously, but with a cool casualness that I found awesome. Where did he put it? And why didn't he show it? The only way I could tell that he was under the influence was that his eyes got a little sadder.

During the weekend of the retreat I sensed him watching me, and after Sunday lunch he suggested we take a walk. I was flattered. Jonathan was a power in the diocese, and I was still in seminary.

We followed a trail through the towering fir trees that led to the overlook where the land just seemed to fall away in a plunge of granite. Standing at the railing, I exulted in the sweeping space—foothills of the Sierra, fold upon fold, and beyond them the violet haze hanging over California's great Central Valley. I could feel the majesty of creation.

But when I turned to Jonathan, wanting to share my exultation with him, I found he was not looking out; he was looking down, and the knuckles on his hands as he held the railing were white with tension. The drop beyond our feet was frightening—a thousand feet, perhaps, down to a churning stream and the pointed spears of treetops.

"Can you imagine yourself falling?" Jonathan said. "Jumping, and for a moment or two being wholly free?"

I shuddered. "I guess we all have thoughts like that, sometimes."

"Do you?"

Our eyes met, and I was uneasy. "Yes."

"The lure of death . . . or freedom?"

"Forgetfulness, perhaps."

"Yes." He considered the matter for a moment. "Forgetfulness. Possibly."

What was all this? A man in his prime. Wealth. Position. A family. Friends. Standing here beside me, contemplating throwing himself off a thousand-foot cliff! But I could look down and know what he felt. Who could he ever tell, this socially prominent investment banker? Where could he ever find a relationship that could fulfill his own gay needs? I could feel myself imprisoned by my own homosexuality, but when I thought of the chains and bars and bolted doors and guards that had Jonathan locked up, I was appalled. No wonder he yearned for just a moment or two of being wholly free!

I felt his hand on my shoulder. "I guess it's the church . . . the faith I have, such as it is . . . that keeps me alive."

I turned to him, and on a sudden impulse, kissed him on the lips. His arms held me fiercely and then broke away. "I'll call you when we get back home," he said.

In the ensuing weeks I kept thinking about Jonathan, hoping he would call. The excitement was consuming. What hadn't happened with Jeremy I determined was going to happen with Jonathan. Jeremy could find warmth anywhere in Mexico, but Jonathan, I felt, was a prisoner for whom I could take some measure of responsibility.

At the same time the excitement was tinged with a titillating foreboding. I could remember the strength of those arms around my shoulders, the desperation, almost anger, of his grasp. I needed him to be gentle. I feared what must be pent up inside him.

Several days after our return from the retreat, he called and suggested we get together that evening. I told him that the next day I was going to be ordained as a deacon. "Well," he said, "that calls for a celebration." I knew and I'm sure he knew that the kind of celebration we had in mind would not have been considered orthodox by the bishop, but I hoped it was going to be an ordination of sorts. Emotional starvation was debilitating, and virginity a burden.

We met, discreetly, at a hotel. I left my car in the parking lot and rode with Jonathan to a dark little bistro where we had dinner. More properly, Jonathan drank his dinner, and I was so nervous I barely got through the gazpacho. Every time our knees brushed against each other under the table, I got an erection, which I chastely hid under the napkin. But the way Jonathan looked at me, I guess he knew it was there.

We talked about the diocese, about the courses I was taking at the seminary, about all manner of godly things. And all the time his eyes were getting sadder.

I wondered how he was going to bring "It" up. I mean, that we were going to go to bed together. Or maybe that wasn't on his mind. Maybe he just wanted some companionship. No, that couldn't be it; he had a wife and kids. Or maybe he expected me to bring "It" up. Like: "Jonathan, I've never done it before, but with you I'd like to try." Or: "Jonathan, I'd like to be your David."

I need not have worried. He drove to a motel as if it were the most natural thing in the world. But he did park the car on the rear side of the motel, invisible from the street.

He was very gentle at first, and I felt the tension drain out of me. This was right for me. This was what I wanted, what I had fantasized about for years. His body was a balm, a shelter, and I nestled in the warmth of it. But as he led me on, his touch grew stronger, and I sensed the desperation in him that I had felt at the overlook.

He had me pinioned on my stomach when the pain came, flashing, electric, coursing through my whole body. I cried out for him to stop, but his response was a guttural gasp—and another bolt of pain. And another. And another. Until tears welled up in my eyes and every shred of sexual excitement had vanished.

Thus he took his angry pleasure on me. I felt unfulfilled and used. If *this* was what it was all about, well, I had better stick to repression, sublimation, and at least heavenly rewards.

Yet soon I was forced out of sexual suppression by the toll that it finally took upon me in terms of psychosomatic illness. And by the following incident, which occurred subsequent to my ordination as a deacon.

Attending another monastic retreat, I made my confession to an elderly monk. Wearing a stole, he sat in a chair before the chapel's altar rail. Kneeling by his side, I quietly blurted out to him that I was a homosexual. (I had said this, of course, in all the confessions I had ever made.) Abruptly he got up and knelt beside me on the floor. He said that I was not to be troubled unduly; I should offer my homosexuality to God, who dearly loved me; and I should faithfully bear my cross.

That night as I lay on my bed in the monastery, I heard a faint sound at the entrance of my cell. A moment later a robed figure stood by the bed. The elderly monk pulled down the sheets and got into bed with me. He placed his arms around me and held me close to his body. I felt no sexual excitement, only a mixture of surprise, fear, tenderness for him, and enormous relief. He accepted me! Some people might want to explain away his loving action by glibly and cruelly categorizing him as "a dirty old man." But his tenderness and gentle grace were angelic qualities to me.

I had known shame and guilt, a sense of despicable ugliness and dirt concerning my sexual condition. Society had taught me to feel this way. The church had whispered secrecy and penance. Yet the beautiful old man accepted me. He used his body to tell me I was loved. Perhaps he felt a need for love also. He simply held me for a long while. There were no words. After he got up and departed, I never saw him again.

Although he helped me, his action was as clandestine as my homosexuality itself. I had lived most of my life on two different planes. I could find no connection between them. I knew that some people who smiled at me, outwardly respected me, and worked closely with me would offer only cold rejection and contempt if they knew the other side of my life. Queer. Faggot. I felt that I could never truly relax anywhere in the straight world in which I lived. I could not ever be myself there.

Yet the monk's nocturnal visit following my confession served as an absolution. It freed me spiritually of my unnatural sense of guilt over my homosexuality. I was at least liberated to live my split life of career on the one hand and my closeted sexuality on the other.

Falling in Love

I went to New York for a year of graduate study at Union Theological Seminary and now began experiencing some sexual reaching out and response. I remember best a sensual, romantic church organist with whom I had the first sexual encounter in which I was able to respond fully. He came to my room in Hastings Hall one afternoon. He had eyes that glowed, a tender smile, and a soft, loving touch. I became intensely excited. But no, he said. We must wait until the next morning for release. I should come to his nearby apartment at 9:00 A.M. Somehow I managed to get through the night without having a nocturnal emission.

In the morning I walked down Broadway past Columbia University, drank a small glass of orange juice and a hot cup of coffee at a counter, and appeared promptly on time at his door. It had been worth waiting for. We made ecstatic love that I found almost unbearably stimulating. But his jealous lover must not find out, he told me, so we did not meet again until years later.

As I had more sexual experiences, I was genuinely surprised to find that a high proportion of gays (including clergy) were married and lived in an outwardly conventional way.

My stereotyped ideas of what it means to be gay started changing as I came to know gays who were hardhats, business figures, professors, clerks, authors, priests, and athletes, various persons in a wide spectrum representing diversified aspects of society. I was astonished and delighted to find that gays were neither merely ciphers nor shadows. Realizing that gays were real human beings like other people, I felt a stirring of hope that I might one day become a real human being, too.

At the age of thirty-three I had an experience that was a watershed in my life: I fell in love for the first time. The first premonition of what was to happen took place in the Union Seminary dining hall. I caught sight of a face across the room. I felt lightheaded and only toyed with the rest of my meal. All I could think was, "He's here."

I had seen that face once before . . . on a windswept road in Germany, where I was attending a Christian youth conference. It was as beautiful a face as I had ever seen, lean, ascetic, with blond wavy hair and eyes that were dark with a brooding sadness. Memling would have rejoiced to paint that face, to capture its quietude and appearance of listening.

We passed on that dusty road. He was with friends, and so was I. There was no way either of us could stop. We exchanged one long look as we passed. I glanced back and saw that he was glancing back. But that was all. And it was the final day of the conference.

I had kept that face in my memory, the presence, the grace of his movements, and the angularities of his body. The remembrance was a kind of benchmark of unattainable male beauty by which all other men could be measured. I had told myself I would never see him again, yet there he was, just a few yards away from me and at the beginning of the academic year.

I caught his eye across the room. Again the same long look, and just the trace of a smile crossed his lips. At that moment, I didn't know what would happen, but I knew that something was about to begin. The excitement was chilling, and so was my sense of utter vulnerability. He could do with me as he would, and I hoped he would be kind.

We met in the Common Room after dinner and fell into conversation as casually as if we had known each other for years. His name was Kurt. He was a German monk, and his accent had a purring lilt and cadence that seemed as intimate as the stroke of a hand. I asked him how he had come to America. He told me that his religious order had sent him for a year's study of liturgics and social action. He was assigned to a parish near the seminary, and he had a room there. After a year he would be going back to rejoin his order in Germany.

Even then I remember thinking, at least we have nine months! It seemed a great gift.

The question was so simply put. "I have some sherry in a friend's room here at the seminary," Kurt said. "Would you like to join me?"

We walked the corridors sedately, my mind filled with garish desire, till we came to the friend's room, a small one like mine, overlooking the quadrangle courtyard. He ushered me in, shut the door, flicked the lock, and turned to look at me with those dark sad eyes. "Malcolm." His voice was barely audible. "Come here."

I took one step toward him as he moved toward me, and we embraced. I felt as if I were in the arms of some shining ministering angel who brought with him assurance of celestial wonder.

His lovemaking fulfilled that sense of wonder in me. I felt gathered and carried beyond anything I had ever known before as sexual communication. This was soul talk of the flesh. I was awed at its depth and radiance.

But lurking there was also a darkness. I felt it in his grasp, where possession verged on pain. I saw it in his eyes; behind the sadness was a hawklike glare that came and went with a flicker of the lids. This angel had seen hell.

Lying next to him, naked, exalted, and fearful, I didn't want to ask the question. But I wanted the pain as I had felt it in his grasp. "Where were you during the war?"

A silence.

"During the last of it . . . Berlin. Medical. Rescue."

"The fire raids?"

"Yes."

I felt a breath of brimstone. Then a horror at who I was. Then a rage at who he was. "You wore a swastika, didn't you?"

The hawklike glare. "Ja."

I rested a hand on his thigh and felt the flesh char under my touch. I pressed my shoulder against his so he would know how it might feel, chilled by a gas-chambered death. And I prayed.

I've written many prayers since then—literate, meaningful to me, and perhaps at times a bit long-winded. But then? It was just a cry of anguish: *Dear God, save us our flesh for each other!*

He buried his head in my shoulder, and the sobs came hard, barking, animal sounds that broke against my skin like explosions. I was embarrassed. This European. This sophisticate. This embodiment of neo-orthodoxy. Crying? On my shoulder? Somehow, everything I felt—everything I felt—rose to this scandalous admission. I pulled his head closer, felt his sweat and his tears, and the sobs came out of me like orgasms, bathing his body with every tear-stained essence I had to give.

The passion subsided. We lay, side by side in a throbbing silence. I thought: I can't handle this. I've got to go. Something. Anything else but this. I can't cope with the whole world. Not in this one angel body. Not in this one small room. I have enough with my own weakling, frazzled self! I have enough just to find God as a friend. How can I find God in the hell fires of Berlin? How can God speak to me through some stranger's penis?

I reared up on one elbow. Kurt said, "What's the matter?"

"I've got to go."

"Where?"

"Back to my room."

"Why?"

"Because . . ."

"Are you afraid?"

I looked at him in the darkness. "Yes."

"I know," he said.

A shaft of light from the courtyard fell on his face. There, I thought, were all the world's agonies incarnate. I could look at its ravages through the eyes of American innocence . . . and arrogance. I knew how distant I had been, and still was, from any profoundly shattering experience.

I fell back on the bed. "Kurt. Love me."

It was a bell-clear autumn day when Kurt and I went together to the Cloisters, the museum of medieval art set high on a bluff above the Hudson at the northern tip of Manhattan. I had been there before and had had a real mind wallow in churchly artifacts. Their setting was so serene, encased in cool stone. Each object seemed to float in a sanitized nirvana, timeless and mysterious. It all seemed so romantic, so medieval. I could prowl the galleries and lose myself among a thousand sanctified spirits, choiring with joy.

In contrast, those remnants of medieval reality that I had seen in Europe seemed heavy with gloom. The Tower of London smelt of blood. Notre Dame deserved a hunchback to keep the gargoyles company. Only Chartres sang. I kept coming back to the Cloisters for reassurance. Now, because I wanted to share everything with Kurt, I wanted to be with him at that place, which represented such exaltation to me.

We walked through the galleries for the most part in silence. Only our bodies kept communicating, never touching, but never far apart. We finally made our way to the outdoor herb garden on a parapet that overlooked the surrounding park, a sweep of the Hudson River and the George Washington Bridge. No familiarity could diminish that awesome view. Kurt was seeing it for the first time.

We stood at the stone wall at the edge of the parapet. Kurt seemed to inhale the panorama as if it were life-giving oxygen, and he straightened to his full height, inches above mine. There was no one else in the garden, and I stood close to him, my hand resting on the stone next to his, and wondered what he was thinking.

Finally he spoke. "I feel like I am coming out of a bad dream."

"What do you mean?"

He gestured over his shoulder. "Everything in there, in the galleries . . . you Americans make it all so different. You bring it across the ocean, scrub it down with Coca-Cola, and set it in a clean stone niche. Anything beautiful. The cross to hold before a dying Albigensian. The stones of a chapel pillaged by the Moors. A tomb of the Black Death. You see only the beauty. Forgive me, Malcolm. I see the history. But out here . . . ?"

His eyes swept the horizon. The breeze played with his blond hair, and he looked like a Viking at the prow of a longboat. "Out here . . . is now. Like you are now. A kind of redemption."

I couldn't say anything.

He raised a long arm and pointed his hand across the Hudson to the Jersey shore, a half-smile on his face as he looked at me. "Out there is Colorado? And Arizona? And all those wild places where you lived?"

"Well, they're a little beyond Jersey, but they are out there."

"Such a grand innocence!"

I felt a trace of annoyance. Was I being typecast as the Noble Savage? "Yes, but I was brought up in New York City, and I've worked in Hollywood."

"Still," he murmured, "so much space to grow!"

Later. That evening. We lay together on the cot in the darkness of my room and peered out the leaded windows into the night scene of the long courtyard below us that was, such as it was, the center of our urban campus. Lying on our bellies, close together, we scanned the trees and lights like a couple of secretive owls, shielded by the darkness inside the room. I slid an arm over his shoulder and nuzzled his neck. He answered with an arm across my waist that moved down to my buttocks. In the silence I felt serenely at peace and secure. The door was locked, the darkness enveloping. Only the vaguest outline of Kurt's face was visible from the lights outside the window. All else was touch and a presence of flesh.

Yet, even then, I tensed and felt Kurt tense, hearing footfalls and voices in the corridor outside the room. As the footsteps faded down the hall, we both exhaled, and I had an urge to giggle, like a kid hiding in a hayloft. But I felt no answering excitement in Kurt. He lay there, motionless. When he spoke, his voice was a whisper.

"You see that circle the driveway makes in the middle of the courtyard?"

"Uh-huh." Hearing his voice, I felt I was about to be told a tale from the deepest of the Black Forest.

"I thought I saw a big stake there, sunk deep in the ground right in the middle of the circle. Around the stake were straw and sticks of wood. Men stood about the courtyard, holding burning torches, the light shimmering on their polished helmets. Then, out the door beneath the chapel, came the procession, chanting. Three cowled figures in black led the way. I think they were bishops—two tall ones and a short one. Who were they? There was something instantly recognizable in the way they moved and held their hands. My God, was it possible that they were . . . ? But then I couldn't be sure, for they wore black masks that hid their faces. They held us, Malcolm, you and me, chained together, wearing only our shorts, with ashes rubbed in our hair and smeared across our faces. The procession circled all around the courtyard, with people leaning out the windows, jeering, throwing things at us—paper coffee cups,

Coke bottles, and half-eaten hot dogs. All around the court-yard the procession went until it stopped in front of the stake. The guards dragged us forward and chained us to the stake, our arms entwined with the metal and each other. The chanting increased, and the jeering from the windows. One of the cowled figures—there was someone extremely familiar beneath that forbidding black mask—held up a cross before our eyes. The short one—yes! now I recognized him—he had taught me ethics in seminary; he had become one of the most powerful leaders of the church—was bowed, perhaps praying for our last-minute repentance. The other tall one—a bishop apparently preoccupied with administration—gave the nod to the guards, who fell away, grasped torches, and put them to the straw beneath our feet as the gargoyles looked down from under the eaves of the roofs.

"We knew it was over. Straining at our chains, we kissed. The crowds at the windows shrieked. The cowled figures put their hands across their eyes in horror. The smoke was merciful. The smoke is always merciful. I learned that on the Wilhelmstrasse. We suffocated in each other's arms before the flames ate our flesh. The ashes where we had stood were collected and thrown into the Hudson River to drift out to the sea.

"The gargoyles were satisfied. See that one, over there just above the light? His ancestors have been watching scenes like that for centuries. But I ask you, Malcolm, why did you Americans have to bring him over to decorate a school building? Why didn't you let him stay in Europe to shatter in the fire raids?"

Kurt's voice, with that Germanic lilt, had been hypnotic, and I had been lost in a vision of some fiery *Liebestod*. Now, suddenly, the gargoyle, the courtyard, the walls of ivy—all so established, so comfortably part of an academic tradition that stretched back to studies of theology at medieval Oxford, Paris, and Bologna—all of it grew sinister, hostile, and foreboding. This was the tradition; this was the arena where heretics and deviants could be scourged from the earth. For loving Kurt, I could be burned. For his loving me, he could share my death. And all in the name of God the Father.

I was trembling. "No. No . . . no! God is my *friend!*"

A silence.

Kurt's voice was sad, almost hopeless. "We lie in bed in a dormitory in the mothering bosom of the established church, which does not know that only a door's width away from its public places we are here, together, practicing abominations. Worse, rejoicing in those abominations."

"We are heretics, aren't we?"

Kurt sighed. "Yes, I guess that does make us heretics."

"Then, how can we . . . ?"

Kurt pounded the pillow with his fist. "I don't know . . . Malcolm . . . I don't know!"

Ever since I had first determined to go to divinity school six years before, I had been skirting the issue, avoiding it, forgetting it, burying it, and hoping most deeply that it would go away. Now, with one stark image, Kurt had defined the issue. It was indelible on my mind, and it would not go away. By the teaching of every church I knew, I was depraved, and what I did was sin. Indeed, the sin was so horrendous that in history it had warranted, with the blessings of the church, man-made death by fire.

During the years in the Berkeley seminary, I could consider my homosexuality my own special burden, a test. It was something to be repressed, set aside, and overcome. "Burn me; burn away the dross!"

But burn away the organist? And now, burn away Kurt? Were they "the dross" that was to be purged from me?

I clung to Kurt's body there in the darkness, as if to shield him from some imagined fire. I felt a sudden rage. If the universe was friendly . . . if God was Love, what right did a church of humans have to condemn and destroy so celebratory a contact between two other human beings?

With Kurt, I now felt that, for me, this was the natural order of things. Now, with Kurt, I felt health flow into me. I could face my own nature and be healed by it.

But out there in the courtyard—I could almost see it—were the gathering figures, and the flames. . . .

I could hear my theological brethren, filled with academic theology and dogma, staring at Original Sin as they would be hypnotized by a cobra, praying for Divine Grace to save them from the inevitabilities of poisoned destruction. They were awed and fascinated by the images of damnation, the circles of hell. I wondered at what circle Kurt and I must, in their minds, be lying. I wondered what they would think, in their Dantean progress downward, if they had found us together and serene in some steaming niche and heard us tell them we'd found heaven. Thus, in our heresy, we would be cut off from the eyes and grace of God.

Bullshit.

Could I not stand, alone before my God, and say, "This is who I am. I can be no other"? Wasn't this the essence of Christianity—a direct and personal relationship between a human being and God? "Listen, for whatever reason you made me, I am part of your creation. I have found a capacity to love. I do not believe that that is sin. I do not believe I should be cut off from your love because of it. I believe that I am fulfilling in my nature what is central to your nature, as revealed by Jesus Christ. I do not want your mercy for this. For other things I need your mercy. For this, only your acknowledgment. Because I believe I am a part—a small part—of your nature. Your act of creation continues today. I am grateful that you permit me to work as a co-creator with you in evolving, changing, sacred life."

It is strange how our consciousness ebbs and flows. Kurt made me brave. That was twenty years ago. We lived as lovers for eight months. Why did it take me another twenty years to write these words? I knew my reality then. Why didn't I just say it then? Out loud, so everybody could hear?

That elderly monk at the retreat, coming to me in the middle of the night and holding me, giving me love and care and absolution for the guilt I felt about my own gayness . . . it had been so quiet, so intimate, so secret. Yet in that darkness it had exalted me and given me strength. He had shared with me the years of his own anguish.

Why couldn't I have stood out there, in the circle of the courtyard at Union, on a warm autumn evening when the students were gathered, and preached under the open sky. "Brethren, let us love one another! And let those of us who wish, love each other in the flesh!" Why couldn't I have given absolution on the steps of the Columbia University library? Or written the good news of myself in any journal that would print it?

I could lie beside Kurt in the secrecy of his room or mine and wonder how many bodies, tormented as mine had been, lay at Union, at Barnard, at Columbia, at Jewish Theological Seminary, and below Morningside Heights in the reaches of Harlem—how many bodies that by word or deed I could have touched, lessened their torment, given them the absolution that that elderly monk had given me.

But I said no word, wrote no word, touched no body but Kurt's, and could feel myself only a part of a secret fraternity of silence. What had been given to me I could not give to others, and, in the last analysis, that was my sin; that was my heresy.

"April is the cruelest month." I lay beside Kurt and watched the green fur grown on the trees in the courtyard. "I want to go back with you." I felt the tears in my eyes. "It can't be any other way."

I thought of the sweep of the hills in Germany. I saw us warmly nestled among the trees, below us the menace and anguish of the world on desolate rock. But we would be safe.

"Kurt, I could join your community."

He rose on one elbow and looked at me in the gathering twilight. "Malcolm, you are a bird. You travel. You migrate from here . . . to there . . . to another place. The members of our community in Germany cannot do that, dear Malcolm. Only the birds can. We know when they come. We know when they go. We never try to net them or trap them. We let them come. We let them go. They are special creatures of God's creation. So are you. You are a bird, Malcolm. You must always be migrating. Always be finding a new space. That is your strength, Malcolm, and your beauty.

"In our community, Malcolm, we have our feet on the ground and work out of stone houses. Would you expect us to fly? Or you to have a year-round rookery in a stone house?"

Was this a benediction or a curse? "I just want to *be* with you!"

The voice was doom in the darkness. "No."

I felt fury. "You goddamned arrogant European!" And I reared out of bed, flailed him with my frustrations. "Coca-Cola, is it? That's all we mean to you? I would contaminate your godly religious community, eh? Just bringing a six-pack of Coca-Cola? With money. And hope. And love. But, oh, no, no! We'd bring capitalist sin with a six-pack of Coca-Cola! I don't deserve the rarefied sanctimony of the community because I'm some vulgar American, eh?"

I knelt down next to the bed, feeling a hatred that was preposterous in front of the one person at Union who encompassed every part of me. But I felt it. I hated that smooth Viking face, that sanctimony of the sin of Berlin.

"I hate your guts, Kurt!"

He looked at me. It was the hawklike look again. "I hate yours, too."

"You Nazi!"

"You capitalist pig!"

"You faggot!"

"You queer!"

A silence.

The laughter came deep out of Kurt's body. "Come here. I want you."

"You can't have me, you son of a bitch!"

"Ah-ha!"

I never knew how strong Kurt was. With a grasp of his hands, I was propelled off the floor and onto the bed. I felt engulfed in his mouth and tried to wrench away. "No!"

I could have saved my silly breath. I was a part of him; he salved my ache; he held me fast. I hated him all the more!

94

And I came, spasm after spasm.

"So, you got me, you son of a bitch!"

He looked up and grinned.

I wanted—oh, yes, with Christian forbearance—to kill him. Why was it that I searched his body till I found him? And triumphed that I loved his flesh? He came. Yes, as resplendently as I had come, spasm after spasm. And just as he had taken me as hungrily as mother's milk, now I consumed him.

I felt our relationship was the one tie I had to my natural being, the one hope I had of God's understanding. I could not live—I thought then—without Kurt. I had the vision of a life in his German religious community that moved with the tempo of the sun and the seasons, the moon and the tides. I was awed by my image of its serenity. Now, with my life too often run by airline schedules, I remember that image and wonder how it would have been with me if I could have been accepted into the community. Then all I could imagine was a life with Kurt, cloistered if need be, but with Kurt.

That was, needless to say, impossible. Our religious responsibilities called us apart from one another. Society did not sanction union between two such people—a priest, a monk, both gay. One wonders: Did society (and the church) prefer hiddenness, shame, guilt, and broken lives?

The day before Kurt was to leave for Germany, we drove to the seashore. We sat down on a rock overlooking the Atlantic. He would be out on the ocean tomorrow on a ship, alone. Above us the seagulls wheeled and cried. We said very little; there was too much to say. I clung to the sense of his physical presence, inches away, and ached as each moment passed. Kurt was leaving—and the body that, in its sensuality, had brought me to a discovery of myself.

In that moment my heart broke. Later, when I read James Baldwin's description of such a good-bye in his novel *Giovanni's Room,* I could identify with it. "I felt a tremor go through me, like the beginning of an earthquake, and felt, for an instant, that I was drowning in his eyes."

I reached out to Kurt. I placed my arms around him. Who cared if a Bible-quoting hater of God's beloved humanity saw us and shrieked unholy invectives? I kissed him on the mouth. I called him "dear" again and again, as I had done many times in the past. I placed my head on his chest. We made love.

The next day, after Kurt had sailed out of New York harbor, I drove again to the seashore. I walked through tall grass until I came to the sand on a deserted stretch of beach. The waves extended as far out as I could see. A few continuously broke in a graceful pattern near my feet.

I lay down on the sand, looked up at the cloudless sky, loosened my trousers, and, with my eyes fixed to the east and thinking about Kurt, I masturbated. The act was a kind of prayer of thanksgiving. For, as I spilled my seed upon the ground, I felt no guilt—only gratitude that, through Kurt and the experience we had had together, I knew my own sexuality and could glory in it.

It was not until several years later that I wrote this letter to the monk whom I deeply loved, a man whom I would have been eager and happy to live with in a covenanted relationship if the church had endorsed such a blessing.

I loved you in a desperate, fresh, urgent way once. You know this. . . . When we could no longer be together, and it was necessary for us to become separated (worlds away), I couldn't walk back into the old world I knew. I couldn't function in the one you had shown (given?) me.

So there had to be a new one. This is what I have never been able to share with you or tell you about. That new world. And what can I say about it now that will really describe it, or myself in it?

We have lived, holding one another in an arrested state of being. I could only assume the crises and decisions, the sadnesses and fulfillments, within your life and never know them. But I wanted to know them. It was the desire for this knowing that I had to relinquish. I finally did.

I love you. What that means, now, for us, I cannot be sure. It is just that I speak to you from my heart. What is my heart? It is where I feel the most tender things, where my life is touched by an ultimate sensitivity. Here, in my heart, I love you. I feel your life tenderly. I am rawly sensitive to your existence. I am not whole without you, so have never been whole.

Soon my work in the church began. At the professional level of helping other people and doing my duties, it moved ahead well. But at the personal level, I could not figure out my identity as a human being. I knew that, as a person who had been created in the image of God, I possessed dignity, meaning, and beauty in God's eyes. But I well surmised that, if society saw the other side of my life, it would recoil as from a leper.

As a young priest of the church I was accorded social prestige and community honor. However, I had to ask myself existential questions. I jotted down these words: "Who am I? Nobody (I feel) now. I am nobody (Is it not so? Surely it is so) when I am lonely. . . . Do I know what life is? what love is? (Am I somebody?) Have I made a mark at all: on a heart, on another life, on the earth, on a piece of paper, on a piece of wood? (Am I somebody?) Yes! Yes, I have! There *is* a heart. . . . "

Gay Bar

In 1957 I was named rector of St. George's Church in the inner city of Indianapolis. It was a lovely church in a deteriorating part of the city that I found infinitely more beautiful than deadened suburbs with their manicured lawns and cookie-cutter people who lacked animation. Around St. George's people were alive—the poor, blacks and whites, prostitutes, ex-convicts, people struggling without pretense against the worst odds to keep going and make sense out of life.

This was a good time for me. I worked hard. I had to be concerned constantly with problems outside of myself. Everything was a struggle, including our efforts to keep the church doors open despite a paralyzing lack of funds. Paul Moore, who was later bishop of the Episcopal Diocese of New York, was dean of the nearby cathedral. Paul, his first wife, Jenny, and I became close friends. St. George's and the cathedral were inner-city allies. Jenny unfailingly helped me by her obdurate hardiness in the face of difficulty or disaster. She possessed an indestructible sense of humor girded by strong faith. Jenny later wrote a book, *The People on Second Street,* about her earlier inner-city ministry with Paul in Newark, and she asked me to write the foreword to it. When Jenny died a few years ago, I was deprived of the loving friendship of a woman who was as close to me as anyone in all my life.

In Indianapolis I soon felt love for another man. He lived alone. He was shy, sensitive, quite a lot of fun to be with, an extraordinarily loyal friend, a creative and innovative person, and someone whose candor and innocence were altogether disarming. His days were occupied in a demanding job. Evenings he often spent in a neighborhood gay bar or else the baths or a bus terminal when he sought a transient sexual partner. I suppose that it was his sheer vulnerability, which he could not disguise, that most endeared him to me.

He could not bear to have anybody stay with him after a climax had been achieved. My desire to engage in slow, sensuous lovemaking with much touching and feeling and to give and receive much lingering affection afterward threatened him. Love, affection, and warmth could never be mixed with sex, he felt, because to him sex itself was evil and shameful. The reality of his worth, his inherent beauty, and his dignity as a person remained a starkly alien figment of a distant theology to him. But how could he have helped feeling this way? A faithful lay member of the church, when he asked for understanding and mercy for his being gay, he met an arbitrary response of disgust and rejection—given coldly and self-righteously in the name of Jesus Christ. Hearing him tell of his life, I could almost feel like Jeremy in Baja California—"on the side of the lions." The sharing of life between us was doomed. Yet I continued to love him.

Friendship with other people helped me during this period. There were the beginnings of long-lasting friendships with a few gays who truly extended me love and understanding. How I envied one happy male couple. Visiting their apartment, I could see the large double bed they shared and a photograph hung on their bedroom wall of two men happily and lustily embracing. And there was the start of a friendship with a nongay friend who has remained very close to me through the years since I moved away.

At that time the only allusions to homosexuality in the press were all negative. I would read about the brutal beating and murder of a priest who was found naked except for a T-shirt. Or about an alleged homosexual involvement of a schoolteacher with a student. Such reports reaffirmed old stereotypes, aroused feelings of hate and self-hate, and denied public legitimacy and acceptance to the gay community. Or I would read about a prominent man who had been arrested on an unverified charge of homosexual solicitation.

The gay bar was an occasional refuge for an encounter with another gay man. The music from the jukebox was loud: "Mack the Knife," "Misty," Judy Garland's songs, or Ethel Merman's. A scotch, a beer. Animated talk, a connection. Risk of entrapment, arrest, or blackmail. Then holding a naked body—ecstasy, release, companionship, *someone* who knew and was known.

The first black person I was ever close to was a hospital intern whom I met in a gay bar. This was when blacks and whites could not use the same public restrooms or eat at the same lunch counter in various parts of the United States, including the euphemistically named Bible belt. But the gay bar was humanly integrated. "This isn't very much like a church, Lord, but many members of the church are also here in this bar," I wrote in *Are You Running with Me, Jesus?* "Quite a few of the men here belong to the church as well as to this bar. If they knew how, a number of them would ask You to be with them in both places. Some of them wouldn't, but won't You be with them, too, Jesus?"

The black intern and I shared one another. God, who had made us in his own image, was with us. But we were hidden from the eyes of a society that would have judged and damned us for who we were as well as for our action of love.

Two Headlights in the Same Lane

After I became a college chaplain in 1959 at Colorado State University in Fort Collins, loneliness continued to drive me to seek gay companionship. I sometimes visited gay bars in Denver and Cheyenne. Gay people in towns across America have had the same experiences I had. In these bars the masks that one wore virtually everywhere else in society, including the church, dropped off. There was a warmth and an honesty in these wonderfully democratic bastions of the outcasts. We had no need to hide our afflictions or our true selves. We could be naked with one another, and in the privacy of motel rooms we were. One can never speak adequately of homosexuality in American society without also considering the social atmosphere that encases and represses it. Many of the feelings and actions that appear to be characteristic of homosexuality are in fact responses and reactions created and shaped by that atmosphere.

In Denver I met a man who worked the counter in a downtown hamburger place. He had dark brown eyes and a hangdog look about him. On a number of occasions we gave each other our bodies, our hunger, loneliness, and mutual need. He had the same ineffable innocence you can see in Giulietta Masina's performance in Fellini's film *Nights of Cabiria*. Both he and she were humble persons emptied of pride, filled with a luminous beauty that the world did not recognize. Neither of them would ever look into a mirror and self-consciously regard innocence there.

We met on Friday nights when we could, had a few drinks, and went to a motel. Our life experiences were different, yet we could talk seriously and listen to one another as we lay side by side awake in bed. When sleep came, we were not alone. Later we awakened to a warm body and a person who cared.

Eventually he went off to the Northwest. Saying goodbye was hard. Weeks later I received a telegram. Could I help him? He had been beaten badly, his small amount of money taken. I wired money. He moved on in an underground world of shadowy people and bars.

My split world continued. Faces, voices, bodies. A night's surcease.

A cattleman I met in Cheyenne had immense shoulders and a rumbling voice. But after sex, he cried.

The beatnik who hitched his way into Cheyenne from Fort Bridges had, indeed, matted hair and a dirty body. But after fifteen minutes in the shower, he emerged like a life study of Raphael's.

I was fascinated by the iridescent transformations that sudden intimacy revealed and have since, in my priesthood, never been satisfied that I knew a person from his or her presence or façade.

My sexual need was strong and demanding. There were some good relationships—one with a gentle, loving man who was handsome, taller than me, and with whom I shared similar cultural and religious interests. We enjoyed one another's company in a casual, low-key way. Once we went to Chicago for a week, rented a cheap room in a nondescript hotel, made love when we felt like it at any hour of the day or night, saw a movie in the morning, ate a hamburger for breakfast or scrambled eggs at 6:00 P.M., and shared warmth and laughter.

One of the least phony people I have ever known, he was direct, steady, and without need of pretense. Our physical sexuality was an unabashed delight; we were able to be open about our mutual needs and pleasures, and I surrendered constraint when I took the initiative in our lovemaking. Yet for us intercourse had numerous forms—quietly talking with each other, sharing stillness, walking, eating, or feeling a strong sense of communion within a crowd of people. We were happy, and he wanted to settle down with me in a permanent life together. However, given my position as a priest in a small western town, the possibility of our making a life openly together was about as great in 1959 as of going to the moon.

One emotionally rewarding experience was with a man I met purely by chance in a bar in San Francisco. He had a reservoir of warmth and tenderness and a most beautiful smile. We shared a lot of ideas and emotions as well as our bodies. Our lovemaking was extraordinarily sensitive and intense. But there was ultimately nowhere to go in each other's lives as closeted people with careers. We both realized this on a foggy morning when we walked across the Golden Gate Bridge, looking down at the ocean waves swirling below us. Our good-bye was unequivocal and sad, as if it were taking place against a flat gray screen.

Similar encounters awaited me in Europe. In 1960 I went to Strasbourg as a delegate to the World Student Christian

Federation conference. A number of us who were gay—delegates from various countries, blacks and whites—related lovingly and sexually to each other there. Afterward, I had a touching experience with a Puerto Rican graduate student in Madrid. Our time together was exquisite, warm, and mutually enriching. We genuinely liked and loved one another, discussing our goals and what we hoped to do with our lives. When I said good-bye to him, I cried.

I realized that I could not keep on indefinitely enduring the intensity of brief-encounter relationships, which drained so much psychic energy without offering any hope of a lasting and more mature human experience. But what could I do? What alternative was there for me? I was not a celibate in my vocation. Nor, as a gay person, was I a candidate for conventional marriage. However, I was a human being with sexual needs and desires to be shared, rooted in a terrible need to give and receive human love.

A surprising amount of my love and sex life remained within the church family. I would be invited to give a guest sermon at a church or a lecture at a college and be assigned to stay overnight with a priest or layman in the area who was, more likely than not, gay—and closeted everywhere but in the privacy of his own home.

We would go through little ceremonies of discovery—a touch here, a look there—and end up in bed together. The number of closeted gay men inside the church astonished me. But, as my knowledge of church life grew to include not just the sanctuary, the rectory, and the classroom but also the bedroom, I began to wonder how much double-standard ethics an institution can tolerate and still maintain its integrity. For example, two heterosexuals living together outside of marriage—including clergy members and soon-to-be-wed new couples following a divorce settlement—were more or less openly accepted without serious moral question. But two gays living together in an announced state of loving union would have been subject to censure. Is the very church itself, Protestant and Catholic, to stay masked?

At St. George's, which was a "white" church, I had tried to establish close relations with neighboring black people, which did not sit well at the time with some of my parishioners. At Colorado State I held religious "espresso meetings" accompanied by bongo drums, which was fine with my student parishioners but incurred the wrath of the bishop. I was soon to be known as "the beatnik priest."

This development was natural for an idealistic young priest whose studies had at one time been guided by one of the great modern prophets of Christian evangelism, Dr. Hendrik Kraemer, head of the Ecumenical Institute in Switzerland. The Christian evangel was to the world, not just to the institution of the church. The blacks were part of the world of inner-city Indianapolis. Those alienated students were part of the world at Colorado State. My job was in the world.

If I had been the most simon-pure heterosexual, I would have probably gone about my vocation in much the same way, given my training and background—except that with me, that vocation had a special intensity, because I was part of a world, too—a hidden gay world.

When the bishop of Colorado pronounced anathema on me for ministering to the Great Unwashed of the Colorado

State student body, he delivered this opinion: "You can't think of yourself as a beloved son of God and at the same time go around with matted hair, dirty bodies, and black underwear" (by which he meant leotards).

In a letter of resignation, I replied: "If a Christian church would ever express contempt of, or self-righteousness toward, any segment of the population racially, religiously, or socially, it would forfeit its claim to be the Body of Christ. A Christian church would deny its dynamic and reason for being if it ever would bar anyone because of a label, be it 'negro,' 'Jew,' 'wop,' 'dago,' 'Catholic,' 'Protestant,' or 'beatnik.' "

I wonder what would have happened if I had mentioned the unmentionable and added the words "or 'faggot.' " But I didn't. I could defend other identities, but not my own. Better to have matted hair and dirty bodies than be a faggot!

So I, antiseptically showered, neatly coifed, decked out in a clerical collar and pressed black suit—I was the most unclean, the ultimate leper. But it didn't show. I was a highly visible public figure . . . but I was an invisible man, who only revealed himself when he chose to in shadowed surroundings.

I could walk the streets in my clerical collar and have old women smile at me and wish me good day. I could sense the deference of shopkeepers. I could see a hand go over the coin box when I boarded a bus. In my collar, I was the church, the repository of goodness and hope. Yet I could feel, beneath the collar, beneath the black suit, that I was caught in a Manichaean dualism of body and soul from which there seemed to be no escape. I yearned for a long-term relationship, the joy of replenishing love that I had known with Kurt.

The early sixties were surging times for the civil rights movement, and I was dismayed at the tepid response white Christians were making to the black demand for equal dignity in a white society.

Hence, after my fire-eating resignation to the bishop of Colorado in 1961, I welcomed an appointment as Episcopal chaplain at Wayne State University in Detroit. In that big, industrial, and multiracial city, I felt I would have an opportunity as a priest to confront the issues of race relations. In addition to my chaplain's duties at the university, I also served as a white assistant in an inner-city black parish. I wrote a weekly column about race relations for the national black newspaper the *Pittsburgh Courier* at the invitation of its Detroit editor, Chester Higgins. I was a delegate to the National Conference on Religion and Race held in Chicago, with Martin Luther King, Jr., as the principal speaker.

Soon after I arrived in Detroit, my photograph appeared prominently in the *Free-Press* and the *News* in conjunction with interviews. I was a well-known public personality, frequently appearing on television. I could not afford to be seen in a gay bar or otherwise provide opportunity for public gossip about my private life. Yet I needed to meet gay friends, embark on a relationship that held meaning for me.

A leading public official in Detroit soon began to court me with considerable charm, aggressiveness, and a no-nonsense attitude. But his gayness was closeted, like mine. So, it seemed to me, we were caught in a public lie with hidden layers of life to deal with meticulously. Never could we be seen as lovers. Never reveal, by a spontaneous handclasp or a look of tenderness across a crowded room, what we really felt. Always maintain the deliberate never-ending choreography of disciplined performers on a public stage.

I realized that this—yet another brief encounter devoid of wholeness and doomed because it offered no serious hope of a maturing open relationship—loomed as a form of death. I ended it.

Several months later, on a speaking engagement in another city, I was given the use of a downtown apartment whose regular occupant was temporarily away. About ten that sleety winter night I was driven back to the apartment after dinner and left alone for the night. Loneliness was gnawing at me, and the pages of the book I had picked up to read seemed meaningless. I decided to go out and have a beer— just one beer. Wearily I walked down deserted streets, the sleet sloshing under my feet, and found a small bar that was open.

Walking inside, I realized it was a gay bar. It was warm, smoky, and noisy, and I happily immersed myself in the pack of people. I nursed my beer and surveyed the mixed crowd. There was a short, cute blond over by the jukebox . . . a romantic Byronic type with longish dark hair two places away from me at the bar . . . and next to him a collegiate number with a pug nose. . . . Then I saw someone who took my breath away, a Moorish prince who had apparently just stepped out of one of those Turkish cigarette ads.

I got next to him and started up a conversation by talking about the sleet. His responses were brief, his look veiled, but I sensed in him the same desperate need, and the same anger, that I had encountered in Jonathan at that overlook in the Sierra.

He came home with me. I made love to him. He tried to respond, and at moments I felt a flooding outpouring of himself as he clutched me. But then he'd retreat into some bastion of hostility, looking at me with smoldering eyes.

I wanted to talk to him. To explain . . . explain what? The only language I could trust was the language of my body, and I flung meanings at him that I barely understood myself. How could I make him understand?

He rose from the bed like a pillar of amber, like an avenging angel—and noticed my clerical collar on top of the bureau. He picked it up with great delicacy. As I stood beside him, he looked at me. "You a priest?"

"Yes."

"Well, how about that!" His eyes suddenly burst into flame. "I don't want to make it with a priest."

"Why? What's the matter with being a priest?"

"I've got no time for the goddamn church. It hates gays. The church hates humanity. The church hates God because God made people. You're a fucking priest in the goddamn church."

I saw the fist coming toward me, felt a crash of pain. . . .

When I regained consciousness, I raised my head and looked around the apartment. Nothing was disturbed, nothing taken. But the room was empty.

Then I saw it, crushed and twisted, lying on the floor—my clerical collar. I was drained.

All night I sat in a chair, gazing into the jet darkness inside the room. What sense was I supposed to make out of being a priest *and* a gay human being? What connection was there between these?

Somehow *I* provided a connection. Inside myself. In my tortured, seeking life. But how was it possible? How?

"Who am I, then?" I asked the darkness.

There was no response out of the heavy silence.

I wanted quite seriously to die. The blackness of the room was transformed, in my imagining, to a twisting road at night. It was raining hard. The road scaled a steep hill. I drove a car. Seated inside it, I was crying.

A car ahead of me moved slowly. I felt that it blocked my way. I must get ahead of it. Even at the risk of meeting head-on a car racing down the other lane, I must have my freedom. I swerved into the left lane—I gunned the car's engine. Furiously I began to race past the impeding car.

But now two headlights in the same lane started to bear down upon me. Could I make it? Could I pass the car ahead of me quickly enough to swerve back into the right lane and avoid a crash? Did I want to be saved? There seemed to be a promising indifference in oblivion, a resolution of permanent peace.

But now the night scene on the highway vanished. I gazed again at the blackness of the room. Was it possible for me to take my life? What would the end be like—a crash, a precipitous leap, or a gentle stillness after a violent drowning? Or I could turn on the gas . . . ?

I didn't close my eyes. The darkness flooded into them. My eyes sought every corner of the darkness. "God, I don't know what to do." My life belonged to—I felt it had a purpose stronger than my compelling urge to destroy it. "Help me, Jesus."

But, I told the darkness, I can take no more oppression. From anyone else or from myself. No more. No more of the flogging and insatiable pain.

The almost imperceptible gray coloring of the approaching morning finally drove the darkness away. I knew I must make a decision, any decision, some decision, about my life.

As a closeted homosexual, I felt absolutely trapped. I could see no life-giving sexual alternatives. I embraced social activism, especially in civil rights, with which I associated the will of God for pressing problems of the world in which I lived. Within a remarkably brief time, my life became an asexual one.

Asexual Years

CHAPTER THREE

Civil Rights Activist

During the early sixties I took part in dozens of demonstrations in the North and South that were part of the civil rights movement to alter American life. The one I remember best was a Freedom Ride "Prayer Pilgrimage" in 1961. I was scared, even terrified. But I felt that if I wasn't prepared to die for what I believed in, what would be the point of life?

Often I faced both arrest and the raw, unpredictable anger of white opponents of racial justice. At public gatherings I met deliberate snubs and sudden, brutal verbal attacks from people who correctly viewed me as an enemy of their way of life. Hate mail arrived by the stack. One scrawled postcard was addressed to me as "Nigger Malcolm Boyd."

As I became an image of a rebel priest and an angry young man, opposition to me grew, especially from various rich and socially conservative church members who did not want their boat rocked.

At this time *Mademoiselle* included me with Federico Fellini, James Baldwin, Jules Feiffer, and Norman Mailer as a "Disturber of the Peace." *Life* named me as one of "the 100 most important young people in the United States" and a member of "the Take-Over Generation." *Playboy* photographed me.

There was deep irony in my public image as an indomitable, even arrogant leader who was fearless, a veritable pillar of macho strength, and a fierce power to be reckoned with by enemies. The truth was that I witnessed out of my faith and conscience, but was personally insecure, was stripped of self-reliance, and experienced an essential lack of confidence in my own power. Still I felt that my participation was the will of Jesus Christ. I did not become an activist simply as a response to my sexual repression.

At the start of 1965 I moved to Washington, D.C. I was exhausted mentally, emotionally, and physically. My sexual desire was at zero, my energy dangerously low.

Yet within a few months I found myself in the public arena as a best-selling author. An ever newer public image emerged. "Boyd is aggressive and articulate, a mixture of inner search and struggle plus outward commitment and self-assertion," said the *Philadelphia Bulletin*. "Not only has he been 'where the action is,' he has, in fact, often been the action." The *New York Times* commented on the "eloquence" and "the personal struggle" contained in my writing, "a struggle to believe, to keep going, a spiritual contest that is agonized, courageous and not always won." I supposed that I had foolishly and inexpertly dropped my mask. However, the *Toronto Star* clearly saw me in a lively mask: "a Marlon Brando kind of face above a clerical collar." The *San Francisco Chronicle* called me "tense-eyed."

Enthusiasm, vigor, and joy drained out of my life as its inner core dried up. I existed only in a rapidly moving, increasingly famous public performance. The stage of my existence burned with bright lights. I knew that many eyes were closely fixed on me as I gyrated, wept, orated, and softly laughed. I was attached to marionette strings. I wondered: Who pulled them? I was so lonely that I could not bear it. More loud applause, with its concomitant of ever-increasing role-playing, only made the isolation worse.

"Malcolm is fast," the *Denver Rocky Mountain News* later noted. "Very fast. For 10 years he spins and fakes and breaks into the open field, fist clenched and the muse throbbing in his heart. The crowd cheers wildly as he sprints toward the goal, but just as he is about to cross the line, it evaporates. Malcolm flashes into a photograph, more, he is photographers' fodder. And, as he stands suddenly alone with a pile of portraits, he says aloud, with a chuckle and a grimace: 'Jesus, I realized that I did not want to be a hero.' " There was more. The *Los Angeles Times* observed, "[He] draws flack like a lightning rod draws zaps." The *Washington Post* described me as "iconoclastic" and a prophet of "a restructured church." The *Cleveland Plain-Dealer* noted, "[His] manner suggests the turbulent waves of the storm breaking over man, church and the American life."

I felt alone in my being. The incredibly life-giving spiritual and human support of loving sexuality would have made all the difference in my isolated, vulnerable life that was under constant fire. I had to manage as best I could to function.

A touch of needed humor was recounted by the *Washington Star*. "It is as the 'espresso priest' that this Episcopalian cleric has become best known," it wrote. "Several national magazines have described how Father Boyd has used coffee house bull sessions ('espresso nights') with students at dozens of colleges to state the case for Christianity. A young man once summed it up this way to a policeman who entered a 3.2 percent beer place in Colorado where students congregated, saw Father Boyd and asked: 'What's he doing here?' Said the student: 'I think, sir, that he's saying good night to his parish.' "

The summer of 1965 found me working as a volunteer in voter registration in rural Mississippi and Alabama. My companions were three young black men who were members of the Student Nonviolent Coordinating Committee. Toughened by strife and outwardly hard men, they possessed a tender vision of justice, love, and true righteousness in American life.

We slept on shack floors out in the countryside, shared food handouts from poor black families, and faced the hostility of the white ruling system, including its police force. The exigencies of sheer survival, as well as the need for energy just to get through yet another day of stark hatred and deadly danger, took up all the slack of my life.

A young blond Canadian volunteer joined us for a couple of days. He was a very handsome, energetic, and muscular man. At night we shared a bed. He lay naked beside me. It was too hot on that southern night to pull up a sheet. The bed was narrow, so our bodies stayed close together.

"Do you ever get lonely here, cut off from so many things you're used to, Malcolm?" he asked.

"Sure. I guess so."

"I'd think you would."

"But it's a whole new life, too, you know, Dan," I said. "Exciting. I never catch up with all I have to do."

"I feel lonely as hell when I'm away from home too long," he said. "You know, rootless or something. Like drifting, I guess."

"Hmm. I know."

"I need to feel that I belong someplace. Connect with somebody. But, running like this, I can't. . . . Malcolm, how do you manage it?"

"What?"

"How do you manage being alone, feeling, well, alone? Running all the time. Jesus, don't you need to feel that you belong someplace—with somebody . . . ?"

Our conversation spun out, then quietly came to a halt. I realized to my amazement that I felt no compelling erotic interest in him, no pressing need to assuage my loneliness or his, no urgency to communicate by more than words. Far more than I'd previously realized, I had entered into an asexual phase of my life. Soon I turned over and fell fast asleep.

Over a period of time I had begun to suffer terrible back-aches. I managed virtually to ignore them, functioning as usual under the brunt of severe agonies that I somehow blocked out of my consciousness. Once when a *Time* reporter came to my apartment for an interview with me, he had to get my feet into socks and shoes—the pain in my back did not permit me to bend over to do this—before we went out to lunch. He suggested that a drink might relax my back. It did not.

The incessant pain in my back, coupled with the fact that I never knew when uncontrollable spasms would strike me there, totally drained my confidence. I withdrew from people and the world, becoming inwardly a sad recluse. But I still crisscrossed the country by plane, filling speaking engagements on many dozens of campuses.

On a given day I would board a flight at Washington's National or Dulles Airport, travel in considerable pain for several hours to a destination, continue by car from that airport to a campus, speak for an hour or two to hundreds and sometimes thousands of people, answer questions for another hour or so, perhaps visit a coffeehouse for a late intimate session with handpicked people, and then fall into a strange bed in utter exhaustion after midnight. My call could be for six or seven o'clock in the morning, for I had to catch another plane either back to Washington or on to a similar speaking engagement elsewhere. My deep tiredness, linked to the unnerving pain in my back, almost obliterated the awful loneliness that I felt during these weeks, months, and years.

Sundays in Washington I functioned once again, as I had in Detroit, as a white assistant priest in a black parish. Otherwise, my social life was nonexistent. I continued to write books, articles, and reviews. Because of my back, I did not usually accept invitations to parties.

Civil rights demonstrations continued to occupy my time and energy. I always considered myself on call for them. Soon demonstrations protesting the growing U.S. presence in Vietnam would involve my body, mind, and soul. Martin Luther King, Jr., was often in the same places at the same times that I was. He was a fearless and warm prophet whom I dearly loved and profoundly respected as a human being.

Writer-Priest at Yale

In 1968 I moved to Yale University to live in Calhoun College as a writer-priest in residence. These were heady days, filled with excitement and pervasive changes in American life. William Sloane Coffin, Jr., who was the chaplain at Yale and a courageous resister of the Vietnam War, invited me to preach in the university chapel. R. W. B. Lewis, the master of Calhoun College, and his wife, Nancy, became close friends. Their house was a fascinating center of visiting writers, painters, U.S. government leaders, and musicians who enriched all of our lives.

I was still trying to keep my gayness hidden even from my own view, and my personal life remained barrenly asexual. Meanwhile, my public life was *very* public. I wrote a great deal, including a weekly column for the *Yale Daily News*. I was a frequent guest on television talk shows in New York, San Francisco, and Los Angeles.

Soon my back worsened. Could nothing be done to make it better? Friends sent me to a doctor in New Haven. He said that he would give me unlimited painkiller pills. But, I asked, what's the matter with my back? Won't you cure the condition? He was unable to answer these questions. I thanked him, declined the pills, and walked over to the Yale gym, where I signed up for a locker. My survival instinct took over. I swam for an hour or so every day after that. This improved my back considerably.

It seems clear now that the repression of my sexual drive and needs and the condition of my back were closely linked. I remember a student friend of mine abruptly saying one day, "If I think I have problems with my studies and wondering what the hell I'll do with my life, all I need to remember is what it must be like to be a queer, a goddamned poor son-of-a-bitch homosexual. Christ, that would be *really* rough."

Whenever anyone, gay or nongay, drew too close to my inner life, I withdrew. What choice did I have? From my viewpoint I had secrets that must remain hidden inside a small, dark closet. The only way they could remain secrets was for me to make absolutely certain never to reveal anything that might cause anyone to suspect the truth.

Every so often, however, I took a small risk. I recall a chat that I had with John Leonard one day in his office when he was editor of the *New York Times Book Review.* We discussed the kinds of books that I might be interested in, and professionally capable of, reviewing. I reeled off a small list of subjects that included books about "religion, social justice, and, well, homosexuality." I had said the word. But surely my eyes revealed no spark of undue interest. I recall the conversation as if it took place yesterday. It is an illustration of the hiddenness in which I believed I must exist. To offer anyone the slightest clue to my homosexuality was a risk not to be taken lightly.

During a visit in New York City to appear on David Frost's television show, I had the worst crisis ever with my back. While taking a bath in my hotel, I suddenly experienced the most excruciatingly painful spasms I had ever known. I cried out, but no one could hear me. It was necessary to get out of the bathtub with its slippery surface. But this meant that I must stand up. The spasms kept hitting me, causing my body to double over in a protective response to the almost unbearable torture. Finally I managed to get out of the bathtub and to my bed. But I could scarcely move or endure to lie there.

I telephoned an editor friend, who came over immediately to see me. Shocked by the deterioration of my condition, he arranged for me to see a doctor right away. Somehow I stood the new agonies of getting into, and sitting in, a taxicab while spasms repeatedly struck my back like bolts of electricity. The doctor helped me by injecting a muscle relaxant into a vein in my arm. But I knew that I would really have to help myself.

On a plane flight to Los Angeles, where I sought help and rest, I occupied three empty seats by lying down across them. A wheelchair carried me off the plane at the Los Angeles airport. In the ensuing days I rested, slowly began to move my body, swam in a pool, and saw a chiropractor, who restored some confidence to me. The combination was a godsend. But chiefly I got my head together. I knew that my back pains were caused as much by emotional and mental factors as by physical ones. Indeed, all these surely came together in the psychosomatic condition in which I found myself. I began to face the reality that I must deal with my own nature in creative and healing ways if I were ever to become well.

The Healing Begins

A long process of healing began. It still continues. It involved my taking strenuous walks of two, three, or four miles every day, come rain or come shine. It meant a long period of twice-daily exercises for my back. Most profoundly, it required me to look into a mirror, see Malcolm Boyd without flinching, and decide that I must not run away any longer from God, other people, or my true self.

The continuing process of my healing took me for long stretches of time to a midwestern town. The celebrity-activist world dropped away from me. I grappled with the meaning of Marianne Moore's words "the cure for loneliness is solitude." Did I find the cure? Yes and no. I identified strongly with Sam Keen's description of his experience with solitude: "A drop of calm, a moment of silence, a thimbleful of the Void is enough to reverse the paranoid movement of the mind."

In the midwestern setting I burrowed into the seasons, coming to know their qualities and moods intimately. I took my daily walks in the snow and ice of winter, brief spring when a seemingly gaunt tree burst for a single spell of days into white blossoms, lazy hot summer that was restorative, and autumn with its sharp reminder of mystery.

125

I reduced the speedometer of my life toward zero. The arrival of the daily mail took on all the significance of a visit from Godot, as I awaited its appearance in a red tin mailbox as if it bore omens from gods. Wrapped in silences, I confronted, and finally became at ease with, the demons whom I had formerly feared and hated most self-destructively.

Vistas outside and inside myself merged in landscapes of stark whites, blacks, and browns. Sometimes flowers punctuated, or even splashed, these landscapes with marks of color. Snow on the ground provided the whiteness for nearly half the year. Trees were black sentinels then; later they appeared to become brown, surrounded by the greenness of their foliage. A few of the trees were among my beloved friends. I talked to them, touched them. More than once I placed my arms around a tree and hugged it.

I fed, and watched, birds. For a time a lively cardinal visited me daily. I felt a closeness grow between us. Then on an ice-cold morning I found its small red body resting in death outside the back door. What could I do as a final gesture of friendship? I carried it into a nearby area and buried its remains beneath frozen winter leaves that lay on the ground. I observed a moment of silent prayer to honor the bird's passing.

Afterward I missed the bird very much. Then on another morning a new cardinal suddenly appeared. I commenced a relationship with it that was somehow an extension of my former friendship with the bird that had died. I also knew squirrels, a chipmunk that was probably a panda in another life, an affectionate and wonderfully lazy black cat, and an extraordinarily loving dog, whose death saddened me.

The dog, its small body riddled by cancer, finally felt too much pain to set its feet on the ground. But one early morning after fresh snow had fallen, I saw it happily run and pirouette for the last time, over cottonlike snow that was soft and free to the touch. The vision of that moment of pure abandon, release, and joy will never leave me. The small dog has a continuing life of sorts here, for its rests secure in a corner of my heart.

During this time I did not interact with many people. There were a few street friends whom I saw occasionally when we engaged in intense conversations about such subjects as meaning, community, loving, hope, and beauty. Every day I visited a small post office to mail a letter, buy a stamp, or simply stop for a few moments of warmth in the icy grip of winter. There were periods when I also visited the public library regularly in the hope of finding a fascinating book or of at least briefly feeling at home among the volumes on the shelves.

What I did, day in and day out, was to block earlier familiar escape routes of my life. I chose to stand firm, working my way through dilemmas and problems by learning how to live with them.

The Yangtze River Under My Eye

I returned to Yale for the year 1971–72 as an associate fellow in Calhoun College. In the spring I visited Israel on a journalistic assignment. Over the next few years I would return several times to Israel, once staying as a guest for three months at Mishkenot Sha'ananim, the creative center for writers and artists located in Jerusalem.

Late one afternoon I stood with a remarkably skilled and perceptive photographer on the rooftop of a home in Jerusalem, watching the sunset. We held drinks in our hands as we looked out over the golden panorama.

"I hate having my photograph done," I said, following up a discussion we had had on the subject earlier. "All my recent pictures are awful. I told one photographer that he should do a maplike close-up of my face for a jacket cover. You know, including the line of the Yangtze River under my eye. He did it, and it was another disaster. Why can't anyone take a picture of me that I like?"

There was a pause in our conversation. Then the photographer said, "Please forgive me if I ask you this question. But maybe it is really the root of the problem. Do you honestly like yourself very much these days?"

The question hit me hard. The truth was that I did not like myself very much at all. I understood then that I had personal homework to do in my life before I sat again for a photograph.

My life was punctuated by extraordinarily meaningful public commitments and occasional high honors. Among the latter was the invitation to prepare and read a paper on "The Law in Perspective of Ethics" at the Bicentennial of American Law conference, sponsored by the law school of New York University. I worked very hard preparing the paper and thoroughly enjoyed the experience, which I shared with Chief Justice Warren E. Burger; Lord Widgery, the Lord Chief Justice of England; Ralph Ellison; Thomas Szasz; A. M. Rosenthal of the *New York Times;* and a number of other distinguished jurists and guests.

But my interior life was a wasted desert. I felt that I was being less and less creative in trying to cope with it. I needed love and sex, together. This combination eluded me.

Certain basic decisions in my life had been made. For one, I would not become an alcoholic. While I enjoyed liquor, and at times it had seemingly met deeper needs of mine, I abhorred its use in excess, was physically unable to deal with bad hangovers, and respected my energy too much to let it be drained this way. Drugs turned me off, for I did not wish to be dependent on them. I kept in good physical condition by walking daily and holding down my weight.

I yearned to make love to someone, and to be made love to, wanting my sexuality to be actively expressed with another loving person. Mere substitutes—whether sex as an impersonal exercise with a faceless stud or masturbation as a form of release—bored me when I realized what I was missing and really wanted.

Hope continued, in a wonderful and mysterious way, to grow in me. Faith remained hard and firm at the core of my being. I understood love in the nature of God, the face of Jesus Christ, and the structure of the Trinity. But still I felt a strong, compelling need to give, as well as receive, love by relating my flesh and soul to another human being. Would my need ever be met? I did not know.

TAKE OFF
THE
MASKS

PART TWO

Coming Out

CHAPTER FOUR

A ll of us are coming out of various closets of our lives all the time," a gay friend wisely said. My coming out as a gay person created headlines and seemed abrupt, yet it was really the culmination of a slow process.

In the fall of 1975 I wrote an article about my gayness. I submitted it confidentially to an editor of a leading national magazine. She responded by saying that as an editor she wanted to publish it, but as a human being she felt that doing so would destroy my "effectiveness" and lead to my "crucifixion."

In December I wrote her a letter in which I concurred with the decision not to publish the article at that time, but also went on to express my deep feelings about the matter:

> Our dialogue has helped a great deal. I am simply continuing it, and am at considerably more peace than I was before.
>
> I don't want *not* to come out because I might be very badly hurt. Do you understand my feeling? I don't want to react negatively out of fear or self-concern about this. Because I am not simply "coming out." It is far deeper than that. Indeed, I fear that my own life and creativity may suffer if I do not have the courage to do what I

should do (though I am not yet sure whether that is to publish or not).

I do believe in Christianity as movement over institution. (Institution is trying to stifle movement.) I want my decision to be "on the side" of Christianity as movement. I want to challenge a false respectability as a cornerstone of a religion based on Jesus the laborer, the outcast, the crucified.

I am antighetto. My whole life has stood for this view. I won't exchange one role (or set of roles) for another without putting up a real fight about it. What I want to affirm is human identity. (Yet, for a number of women and men, it will be necessary to work through questions of gay identity in order to get to human identity.)

I feel much more relaxed (that funny word) and can see the humor of it all—the human enterprise with its marvelous warts, colors, differentiations, and absurdities—and the self-righteous way people have of looking at each *other*. Simply to be God, God must have the greatest sense of humor in all the world.

I am able (I think) to take "risk." Doesn't truth have to be honest risk? I guess I'm willing to stake my reputation and future livelihood on the likelihood of a decent and thoughtful response from people—especially if sensationalism can be eschewed and notoriety shunned wherever possible in favor of good-spirited discussion and high-principled treatment of an aspect of the human condition.

I don't want to "go to the grave" without telling my story. This means that I believe strongly in history. Frankly, I'd prefer to engage in the discussion myself—not have it be merely "about" me. In an ongoing dialogue (albeit with healthy controversy) the discussion grows and develops. I'd find that immensely interesting, challenging, and useful.

What's interesting, and perhaps valuable, is that I am neither an established homosexual nor a young street stud, a publicized militant gay nor a social gay stereotype. I am a religious figure of my time, a member of a prestigious institutional framework, an author with a following, a well-known American. (And this happened to me!) It could be important in total honesty and truth to try publicly to figure out "why," as well as what I should "do" about it, what are its personal and social ramifications, what does society want or expect of me, what do I want or expect of myself (and society), indeed, what are my precise responsibilities in terms of this reality in my life.

Although the article in which I wished to divulge my gay identity did not appear, obviously I was seriously wrestling with the matter of my decision to come out of the closet.

I did come out to a few individuals. One was a close friend, Lynn Caine, author of the books *Widow* and *Lifelines*. One evening I was seated across from her on a sofa in her New York City apartment. I said that I had something very personal to tell her. Lynn inquired what it was. I paused.

She moved over to sit next to me and took my hand. "What is it?" she asked again.

"I don't know how to tell you," I said. "I'm, well, I'm— it sounds so odd, doesn't it?—homosexual. I'm gay. I'm gay, Lynn."

She held on to my hand and said, "I always knew that, Malcolm. Why didn't you tell me before, darling? It's wonderful that you can finally say it . . . and about time! . . . Don't you know that I love you?"

Reactions from a few other close friends were similar in kind.

At that time, when I wished to purchase a gay newspaper or magazine, I would never approach a newsstand and ask for a copy. I would either find a newspaper vending machine on a street and insert a coin for a copy, which I promptly folded to hide its identity, or else would walk up to a newsstand and buy a half-dozen or more publications—casually including the gay one in the group. I was absolutely paranoid about going openly up to any news vendor, picking up a gay publication, and paying for it by itself. Good Lord, doing so might indicate to someone that I was *gay*.

But I took a step toward personal liberation when I decided to cut off a lock of hair on the front of my head that had disguised a bald spot (except when it blew out of place, which it did on numerous occasions, causing my vanity to suffer irremediably). I also grew a mustache—a giant step for me, although this probably sounds totally absurd to anyone else. It meant that I had made a liberating intimate decision about my appearance, my self. I changed the first. I deeply wanted to change the second.

Soon I received two speaking invitations that spurred my decision to make a public announcement. The first was to deliver the sermon at the ecumenical religious service of Chicago's Gay Pride Week in June 1976. The second was to give the keynote address at the second annual Integrity convention of gay Episcopalians and their friends in San Francisco in August. Neither invitation implied that I was gay or called for my coming out. I accepted both. I had long expressed views on other aspects of the human condition and their relation to Christ's gospel in the contemporary world. Now the time had come to address the gay condition.

Chicago's Gay Pride Week religious service was held at dusk in a park by a lake. There were songs and readings by representatives of various gay caucuses, Christian and Jewish. Readings were from the Bible and also *Boys in the Band* by Mart Crowley, *Rubyfruit Jungle* by Rita Mae Brown, *On Being Different* by Merle Miller, and *You Are Accepted* by Paul Tillich. Readers represented Congregation Or Chadash, Metropolitan Community Church, the Methodist Gay Caucus, Lutherans Concerned for Gay People, the Presbyterian Gay Caucus, Integrity, and Dignity. In my sermon I preached about God and gays, but did not publicly come out. Previously I had asked close gay friends what I should do about coming out on this occasion. They had said it could seriously damage my usefulness as a priest and that I should not do so. After the sermon I embraced and kissed a number of gay women and men at the service. It was a moment of high emotion, and I came out to several individuals there.

Just a few weeks later I was in San Francisco to be the keynote speaker at Integrity's convention. Once again, because of the advice of gay friends, I had not planned to come out publicly. Yet at three o'clock on the morning of my address, I awakened, got out of my bed, and added a few sentences to the manuscript of my prepared speech. They constituted a public statement that I am gay. Several hours afterward, my address in Trinity Church was greeted by an outburst of emotion. I felt happy and relieved of a burden that I could no longer carry alone.

Following the speech, I engaged in a freewheeling question-and-answer period over lunch with delegates to the convention. The mood was very high and relaxed. I spoke

with candor about my gayness in the context of responding to a wide variety of questions.

That night a young priest from Michigan, a delegate,
and I went dancing at a discotheque—dancing with release
and joy at the deafening music that exploded rhythms deep
in my subconscious self. I had the time of my life, and this
surprised me. A short time before I would not have dreamed
of doing such a thing. I was uptight about my body. Also,
my sense of propriety would have ruled this out of bounds
for me. Now my body moved to the beat of the music and
the rhythms of my partner's body. From time to time I enjoyed following him as well as leading. This, too, would
have been incomprehensible to me before. My whole personality would have shouted down such an encroachment
on my macho needs.

The *Advocate,* the national gay newspaper, assigned Dean
Gengle, one of its editors, to cover the Integrity convention.
A few weeks later my coming out became more public
when the *Advocate* front-paged "the gospel according to
Malcolm Boyd." It quoted me as saying, "In civil rights I
was arrested frequently, despised by people who had formerly honored me. As it happened, my fragmented life was
becoming unified. The pieces were coming together because they had to. It was God's insistence. That's when my
sexuality came into focus. I had to work with it and through
it, and look at it, experience it, figure out what it was and
what I felt about it. My sexual development, in other words,
has grown and been a part of my religious experience."

Yet even now I had not come out to most of my friends
and the general public. A month later I visited Chicago.
One evening I had dinner with Roy Larson, then religion

editor of the *Sun-Times,* and his wife at a Latino restaurant in Evanston. Dorothy Larson asked me if I was married and had children. I said no. The conversation moved on. For what had seemed the last hundred years, I had always routinely answered no to that inevitable question. And I had done it again this time. But in a moment I said, "Excuse me, but I want to go back to something I said. You asked me if I am married and have children. I'm gay. This doesn't mean that I couldn't be married with a family, but I don't happen to." A certain Rubicon had very quietly, but very definitely, been crossed.

I decided to follow that private revelation with a public declaration. It would appear the following Sunday, September 12, in the *Chicago Sun-Times,* in an interview by Roy Larson, one of the finest religion writers in America as well as a person of unquestioned integrity and taste. The time had come, I felt, for an end to ambiguity in my life.

While I felt enormously relieved by the prospect of being known at last openly by everyone, yet I suffered deep apprehension about the pain that my announcement might cause a number of people close to me. Would my coming out rupture or permanently destroy our relationship? I had only three days to wait and find out.

These were exceedingly busy days. I had come to Chicago while engaged in a two-month nationwide search for examples of creativity and hope in American religious life. So my days, and parts of my evenings, too, were fully occupied by interviews with dozens of people in various sections of the metropolitan area, from the inner city to distant suburbs. My unrelenting work assignment allowed me little time to think about my own coming out except when I lay in bed at night and listened to the ticking of a clock and my own heartbeat.

On Saturday I had scheduled an interview with a Lutheran pastor at his church located in a suburban shopping center. When our conversation was completed and I returned to the city by train, the early Sunday edition of the *Sun-Times* was already on newsstands along the streets.

I did not want to open the paper and read the story alone, so I caught a bus to the apartment of the gay friend with whom I was staying. (A member of Integrity in Chicago, he cannot be mentioned by name here because public identification of his gayness would probably cost him the job that he has worked hard for many years to protect.) When I reached the apartment, my friend was there, the *Sun-Times* stretched wide open at his feet. "Kid, you're out," he said.

The headline read: " 'I'm gay,' declares Father Boyd, the fighting priest." The story said I had entered a new arena of controversy by publicly declaring my homosexuality. "I don't want anything more to do with masks," the interview quoted me. "I'm gay. In saying this, I feel secure, unthreatened and happy. It's something I felt I needed to do."

A human tidal wave of reaction struck me within a few hours. The story was carried on the press service wires. It was seen and heard on television flash announcements, in newspapers, and over radio stations in every part of the country. Magazine and newspaper reporters were soon on the phone for further statements and interviews. I sensed instinctive human support rather than hostility or rejection.

The first telephone call came from Frank Deford, a friend of mine who was then a senior writer for *Sports Illustrated*. He had read the story in a New York newspaper on a plane en route to Dallas. He said, "Gee, I don't know what to say. They don't make Hallmark cards for this." We both laughed and relaxed.

A few close friends were profoundly shaken by my announcement, and there ensued hours-long telephone conversations full of tension, anger, and pain. These were matched by other conversations full of joy, release, and happiness. I felt a bit like a leaf in a windstorm.

"I repressed my own feelings for a long, long time, thinking God viewed homosexuality as ugly, demonic, and sinful," I told journalist Linda Witt. "Now I know it's beautiful and God loves it." This prompted a three-page letter from a friend filled with Bible quotations making the point that God does not accept (or literally damns) gay people. But the letter writer communicated with me the following Christmas once again. Couldn't we, after all, remain friends? Yes, of course, I replied.

Such initial responses, however, created some feeling of paranoia in me. Did friends and acquaintances virtually everywhere accept me as gay in the same way that they had accepted me before? I did not know. When certain friends did not communicate, I sometimes assumed harsh judgment on their part. This was unfair of me.

The following Christmas, with its outpouring of expressions of love on many cards, proved to be a reassuring and healing time. Then, given a fresh perspective, I realized that I had no right to judge my friends—or anyone else. For some of them my coming out was perhaps as difficult in certain ways as it had been for me.

I have never heard from a few close friends. Were the horrible stereotypes of gays so strongly fixed in their minds as to preclude acceptance of me as a gay person? Or was there resentment that I had been unable to share the reality of my sexuality with them, despite our candor and intimacy concerning almost every other subject? Possibly they did not realize that I was *really* unable to come out until I did. This fact cried out to be understood in our relationship. But now I felt, rightly or wrongly, rejection or resentment coming from them, and it hurt me quite badly.

For other friends, my coming out was simply a matter of my having stated publicly what they had always assumed, or another fact of life to be coolly lived with, or even a matter of relative indifference amid the plethora of life's complexities, including their own special problems. Most of the Christmas cards carrying expressions of love made no explicit reference to my having come out of the closet. I appreciated in a special way the few that did. One, addressed to "Dearest friend," said, *"Boyd says, 'I'm gay!'—Is that for real?"* So, we could talk about it. It helped.

Certain friends made no reference to the matter in our first conversations after the announcement. This caused me to feel unrelaxed with them. I felt that I had nothing further to say about the subject at that moment, so it went unrecognized between us. I appreciated a friend who said, after we had talked over the phone for a short while, "We saw your announcement. It couldn't have been easy to do. We want you to know that we love you and are your friends."

My coming out was difficult for my eighty-year-old mother. The occasion also meant, finally, coming out explicitly to her. She is a remarkably loving, disciplined, and committed woman, whom I described this way in *Am I Running with You, God?*

She knows how to cure the common cold by rubbing goose grease on one's chest; prepare a memorable pot of vegetable soup (based on *her* mother's recipe) that cannot be bought with gold in the finest restaurants of New York or Paris; care for the birds that flock to her backyard, tend a rose garden, manage her home; keep up with reading, correspond with friends everywhere, work as a volunteer at a children's hospital; study French and the guitar at a nearby Everywoman's Village; paint, design her Christmas cards; heal backaches by a massage with oils; cherish the company of two faithful dogs; swim six months of the year, reject any onslaughts of depression; dress in impeccable but understated fashion—and always wear a ribbon in her hair; remain loyal to old and new friends, speak her mind directly if sometimes bluntly, care deeply about social issues, volunteer to assist political candidates of her choice; laugh on occasion at herself and everybody else, and show the world a stubbornly happy and smiling face.

However, my mother's views of homosexuality were, it seemed to me, stereotyped ones, the result of religious clichés and media carbon copies. Homosexuals? They were shadowy creatures whom one could pity but did not know as flesh-and-blood people. Her son a homosexual? Impossible! Upon my coming out, and for months afterward, we failed to communicate satisfactorily about the subject. My efforts to introduce her to people, or even books, as agents of consciousness change were unproductive. Her efforts to relate to me as I was formerly also met with failure.

Yet our relationship held firm. We were not only mother and son but also friends. I never doubted her unyielding love, nor she mine. We mutually agreed that we were unable to comprehend one another's feelings concerning my being gay, which included openness on my part and a new lifestyle. Tenderly and with deliberate intent, we moved away from harsh confrontation on issues that left us both shaken and hurt badly. We allowed time to do its healing work and cooperated with it in every possible way.

Being in the midst of supportive people seemed to save my life when I came out. There was always the assurance that I was loved and accepted as a human being, however much I moved against the accepted mores of society. In the center of public conflict I did not have to face my problems alone.

My immediate gut reactions were caught expertly by *People* magazine. "Jesus was despised, flogged and spat on," I said. "I'm happy to be able to do something for fellow homosexuals who are despised, flogged and spat on." I went on to say that I had developed "a growing awareness of my gay friends who were priests and bishops and nuns and monks. It was a gradual acceptance of them. Then I realized I was them."

Yes.

I did not want simplistic, unqualified approbation from people by way of response to my public action. I have never either wanted or honored such banality. I sought honest responses. One that I especially appreciated came from a seminarian who wrote, "In all honesty, although I am not in favor of your position, I believe that we must move beyond our 'gut level' reactions to a much more informed opinion. Your openness on the issue of homosexuality is both very courageous and honest." Another seminarian wrote, "You have a lot of guts to let your truth be proclaimed. While I will take a while longer to be comfortable with the revelation of your sexuality, I am thankful for your ministry of honesty."

Sexual differences, like other signs of uniqueness in our lives, need to be celebrated, not castigated. I like what Peter Shaffer, the author of the play *Equus,* said in an interview about being different: "No one can contemplate a mass society in all its banality and barbarism without being worried. Particularly if that society is held up as a norm. If you were to ask me if I'd like to be 'normal'—being defined as someone acceptable to a mass society—I would say, 'No, I would not; I'd rather be as far removed from that as possible.'" Why not peel off our skin, if need be, in order to be ourselves? It may help others to be themselves, too.

I felt that a great deal of dialogue was opened up where it did not previously exist. Of course, some previous dialogue, or the semblance of it, ceased. This seemed to be the case with a handful of religious leaders who quietly vanished from my life. One nationally known leader, however, communicated with me quite poignantly. He informed me in a short handwritten letter that he was gay but would probably feel constrained to remain always in the closet. I telephoned him. We expressed love and support for one another in the different ways that we believed we had to follow.

Following a church service in New York City at which I had been the preacher, a man quietly announced to me, "I am locked in the closet and must stay there." One can never make a decision about coming out for another person or judge that person's own decision. Yet I told him,

"While I completely accept your staying in the closet and give you my love and support, I don't feel that you should be *locked* in it."

Four days after the public announcement of my coming out, I was scheduled to give a speech at a Jewish conference in Wayne, New Jersey. When I flew into Newark for the appearance, a friendly young public relations man smiled easily and told me, "You've been in the news this week." I agreed that this was true. "There's a press conference scheduled for tonight," he said. "You and the other speakers are expected to participate in it."

The other speakers included Uri Ben Ari, consul general of Israel in New York; Professor William Korey, director of the B'nai B'rith United Nations office; and Rina Messenger, Miss Israel and Miss Universe 1976. The press conference passed without my being asked any personal questions. My speech to the two thousand people attending the conference received an ovation. I realized that my life would go on in various familiar ways, although a radically new dimension had been added to it, and it would certainly never again be the same as before.

A few days later I taped an interview at NBC-TV in New York. The interview was about another subject. No personal questions were asked. Yet I felt that many eyes in that television studio were looking at me in an altogether new way—that for them I was "a homosexual" now, an image of sexuality, not merely the priest-author of previous appearances.

Instinctively I identified with the journalist portrayed by Jack Nicholson in Antonioni's film *The Passenger,* who assumes the identity of a dead man he resembles. Immediately he has a new passport, a new identity, but also even new skin. He has become someone else whom he does not know at all. It is a curious heady experience that carries him into new relationships and experiences and, as a result of the switch, ultimately to his death. For several weeks I felt that I was moving on unfamiliar ground through intricate new phases and steps. I did not know where I was going. People were responding not to "me" but to an image that seemed a stranger. I thought of what Ralph Ellison wrote in *Invisible Man:* "It is as though I have been surrounded by mirrors of hard, distorting glass. When they approach me they see only my surroundings, themselves, or figments of their imagination—indeed, everything and anything except me."

A lot of people responded to me as a person, showing this in kind, gentle, thoughtful ways. But there was tension in the air. It seemed that a new ingredient had been added to my life and everyone's response to it. This was exciting and demanding. My new experience required more psychic energy than I felt anyone could possibly realize.

I read with wonder Jane Hamilton-Merritt's description in *A Meditator's Diary* of really *seeing* an orange for the first time: "I saw the saffron brilliance of an orange slice held together with the most delicate of fuzzy gossamer threads with three wet quaking bubbles of translucent juice." Would I ever be able really to *see* life's beauty, sensuality, and reality this way? I wondered: Could I openly sleep with a lover gently, tenderly, sexually, as a genuine part of love? Loving. The body. The mind. The soul. The needs of these. The body's sweat and ecstasy. The struggle to be human and belong and love another person freely, responsibly, and unselfishly.

I desired to share the wholeness of my life. I could not feel truly whole if something so elemental about life and existence on earth as loving could not be openly shared. Although I am made in God's image, yet I had long been told by the church and society that I was sick, half of a real person, damned, unstable, dirty, and evil.

My liberation lay still ahead of me. I had fought for the liberation of many other people, yet I had not been able to share the reality of my own personhood in otherwise close friendships. Christ died for me. I gratefully accepted this. Could I live for Christ in the full brilliance of light? Could I live with, as well as for, others—receiving from them, and sharing with them in my raw need, not being just the paternalistic giver?

Reactions to my coming out represented a wide spectrum of viewpoints. The wife of an Ivy League university professor said that, in her opinion, I clearly felt the need to embrace an ever new cause. First, there had been blacks, followed by the peace movement. Then, she noted, I embraced the causes of women and Jews. Now—it was gays. Someone else, in a similar vein, expressed the view that I was apparently fascinated by minorities. A minister in New York City said that I was a liberal who simply jumped on the newest bandwagon. An editor said that I had come out of the closet in order to have a new public platform. A seminary student said that I was to the avant-garde as a moth is to a flame.

How did I respond to these reactions?

First, *is* it a bad thing to seek to balance the personal dimensions of the gospel with socially outreaching ones?

"Thou shalt love the Lord thy God. . . . Thou shalt love thy neighbor as thyself." These two great commandments constitute the love ethic. I do not apologize for my efforts to honor them that way.

Second, I *am* fascinated by minorities—especially when I am a member of one. I have long held an outsider's view of society. I have been a consistent critic of established social patterns.

Third, injustice is not a new bandwagon. Had I lived in Nazi Germany, I earnestly hope that I would have had the depth of faith and conviction to support the cause of Jews against fascist death camps. The cause of blacks is not a new bandwagon; it is *the* American dilemma, as old as the nation itself. The causes of women, of Jews, of peace are ancient and lasting ones.

Approximately a quarter of a million gays perished in Nazi death camps within my lifetime. Alas, millions of American gays live incomplete lives in shadows. "Young gays need a sense of identification. They don't get it because their models are locked in the closet," wrote Wallace Hamilton in *Christopher and Gay*. Countless gays' jobs remain in permanent jeopardy, their lives wrapped in seemingly necessary secrecy, their potential loving natures still scarred and warped by the presence of a haunting process of persecution.

Yet gays are part of the total American culture and can be found in all segments of it—the army, the church, the arts, government, Harvard, labor unions, Wall Street, Hollywood, and football. A group of Christian gays announced in a denominational church convention in the Midwest, "We are your brothers and sons." Even Archie Bunker, along with millions of his television viewers, discovered a male gay in the guise of a middle American beer buddy in a neighborhood tavern. It is tragic when religious Mc-Carthyism exerts a self-righteous and arrogant tyranny of politicized fundamentalism over the human rights of a scape-goat minority. But the closet door is open.

It must never be shut and locked again.

Masks

CHAPTER FIVE

Marlene Dietrich has long been a favorite personality among gays. I was surprised and delighted one afternoon on arriving in Atlanta to see a poster in the hotel elevator announcing that Dietrich was beginning a series of appearances that same evening in the hotel cabaret.

I called the maitre d' and asked if he had room for a single reservation. He said yes. I entered the lounge shortly before the first orchestral downbeat of opening night. It was embarrassingly near empty. When I was ushered to a ringside table, it was not out of kindness but out of a need to fill the space in front of the stage.

Dietrich looked marvelous. Her body and legs were in splendid shape, her gown a reminder of past glories in Paris, London, and New York. But a young woman seated at the next table loudly asked her expense-accounted businessman escort for the evening, "Who *is* she? What's her name?" I hoped that Dietrich did not hear her.

The songs were good in the way that a fire of embers can be on a cold night. I wondered why Dietrich continued to work so hard, tour the provinces, push beyond her obvious limits, and open herself to the fiasco of an empty house. Maybe she needed the money. Or maybe continuing to perform was like oxygen for her.

I led at least three standing ovations by the simple expedient of getting to my feet and shouting, "Brava!" The remaining few people, including the young woman at the next table, followed suit.

When the performance was over, I leisurely finished my drink and walked through the hotel lobby to the elevator. I was filled with a sad passion at having watched Dietrich step out of her elegant past into a harsh present of shabby neglect. My passion had been nourished by two drinks. And here before my eyes in the elevator was the poster of Dietrich, a reproduction of a splendid drawing of her face. I must have it. Surely, I reasoned, the hotel had dozens of these posters in stock. Indeed, the management probably would be grateful to me for taking it as a kind of advertising of the event. So I mused.

I reached for the poster and pulled hard to detach it from its frame. It did not yield. I pulled harder. The poster came loose in my hands. But at the same moment the wild sounds of hell seemed to explode. Apparently there was an alarm system linked to the poster frame; deafening sirens as if from a dozen ambulances, combined with eruptions as of volcanoes, barraged my eardrums. Holding tightly on to the Dietrich poster, I broke into a sweat. Had I committed a terrible crime? My heart pounded furiously. Was I losing my mind? I was terrified.

The elevator reached my floor, and the automatic door opened. I looked down the long passageway toward my room. The sounds were still exploding all over the place. A couple of doors in the hallway were opened a crack by curious or frightened tenants. A man stood in a doorway attired only in shorts, his eyes wide in disbelief. They saw me streak down the hallway at full speed, stand shaking outside my door as I clutched the Dietrich poster in one hand and tried to find my key inside a pocket with the other, finally get the door opened, rush into my room, and slam the door behind me.

I stood in absolute silence on the other side of the door inside my room, listening for sounds of approaching police, waiting to be seized and carried off to a cell.

After quite a while I decided that apparently I was not going to be arrested until the next morning. I placed the Dietrich poster facedown in the bottom of my suitcase. After untold agonies I managed to fall asleep.

I was not seized. The Dietrich poster graces my desk. The sketch on the poster is a lovely mask of a favorite star.

Alas, not all masks are so lovely. When I came out of the closet and announced in Chicago, "I don't want anything more to do with masks," I meant it. I was familiar with masks, including my own, all too well. The public knew me in three principal roles. They knew me first as a religious figure seen frequently on such television shows as "Today" and quoted in newsprint; second, as a social activist in civil rights and the peace movement as well as an oft-quoted social critic; third, as the author of numerous books, including *Are You Running with Me, Jesus?*

So, while I was widely known—even (ironically, in my view) being included in the *Celebrity Register*—yet I felt that I was not really known at all as a human being. "Trying to interview Father Boyd is like trying to kill mosquitoes with a slingshot," the *Toronto Globe* said.

I was a collection of masks in public—a face in a newspaper column or on a television screen, a quotation in newsprint. One can know very little about any public figure on such a basis. May I provide you with some real connections between the Malcolm Boyd whom you thought you knew and the one I know?

You see, as a writer, I had masks with holes to see through. How many people ever saw my gayness there? Let's take a look at these writings and what they reveal about me as a person who is human and also gay.

My first three books contain very few holes to see through. My masks were tightly in place. However, *If I Go Down to Hell,* my fourth book, and *The Hunger, the Thirst,* my fifth, contain clear clues pointing to my experience of homosexual repression, sadness, and guilt. The former is filled with cries of loneliness and longing for relationship and contains disturbed poems.

In *The Hunger, the Thirst,* I noticed that within the hearts of some people there are "cobwebs, shadows, nightmares, hates, labyrinths of lost and broken dreams, old price tags and fragments of old receipts, and nothing, nothing, nothing, nothing." I wrote the following words out of my terrible need for a better and happier life: "We want neither to be stereotypes or personalities but persons. We all experience the yearning that the world of one moment, absorbing all of oneself, might be related to the other worlds absorbing oneself in other moments. We all hunger, at one time or another, that the small, whirling universe of self might be able to communicate in transparency of truth and strength of relationship with the small, whirling universe which is another life."

Ironically, my next book was the enormously popular *Are You Running with Me, Jesus?* which created a new public stereotype and personality for me. The book, containing eighty-nine short prayers, was published in November

1965. Five months later the *New York Times* lauded the prayers as "very moving . . . terse, slangy, always eloquent." Twelve months following publication the book was a runaway best-seller. Seventeen months after its launching, the book was hailed by the *New York Times Book Review* for its "blushing honesty and piercing ethical directness." The mood of the sixties had a lot to do with the book's growing reception. This could not be separated from the immediate post-JFK spirit of hope, the Peace Corps, civil rights, and a strong consciousness of youth's potential to bring about deep changes in American society.

The need to write the book came from my own problems with prayer. Wasn't God supposed to be *up there?* So, the words traveled up to him. This neat system collapsed for me. I virtually stopped praying, except for using the Lord's Prayer.

In the spring of 1964 a group of Roman Catholic laypeople and a few priests invited me to visit Israel and Rome with them. We stopped on the island of Cyprus. One day as I lay on my cot, trying to pray, I picked up a ballpoint pen and a notebook and wrote the prayer "Are you running with me, Jesus?" which would be the first one in the book.

The prayer about a gay bar in *Are You Running with Me, Jesus?* brought me my first letters from gay readers. One poignantly thanked me for identifying God and prayer with the condition of being gay.

My gayness made me identify with the light and darkness, the highs and lows of the Psalms, and the cry of Jesus from the cross: "My God, my God, why hast thou forsaken me?" As a gay person, I knew at the center of my being that the sacred and the secular are truly knit together, the holy being inseparable from what is "raw, naked, in the best sense 'vulgar.'"

My mask was full of holes to perceptive readers of *Are You Running with Me, Jesus?* Surely I stood naked to those who had eyes to see. Yet how many did? My next book was *Free to Live, Free to Die,* described by *America* as "aggressive, disturbing, in fact subversive." The *Chicago Tribune* called it "a drama of redemption." It was angry, antiestablishment, intensely personal. *Book of Days,* following it, was even more so. This book asked the question "Isn't it blasphemous to say you take Jesus Christ with you into a homosexual bar?" I was vulnerable when I wrote, "There is a small grain of terror somewhere inside me. I'm frightened that it might grow, absorb other particles of myself, and overcome me. Some day I may find no solid ground on which to move, or feel, or relate. I may just sink down." The *Atlanta Journal* observed, "[Boyd] sometimes comes on like a Feiffer cartoon."

In *The Fantasy Worlds of Peter Stone and Other Fables,* I had a seasoned newspaperwoman ask a seminarian who portrays Jesus in a multimillion-dollar film, "Do you think Jesus was homosexual, Mr. Stone?" A year later, when I wrote *As I Live and Breathe,* I was not yet prepared to come out, so I was unable to deal explicitly with my homosexuality. But I wrote, "Now I hear a motorcycle, now guilt; a jet races overhead and a compulsion to be free on the periphery of what passes for my heart." The *New York Times Book Review* correctly noted, "It may be Boyd's autobiography, but it is really a story of our times. The vibrations of church and society and race and war are so tightly interwoven that you can never separate them." Exactly. The book is not my story from a personal standpoint so much as the definitive chronicle of my public experiences.

Gay heads poke through the windows of several other of my books. A man described as "thirty-five, good-looking, active in public life, and homosexual" appears in *Human Like Me, Jesus*. Paul, who "waits to visit a gay bar" and sometimes "makes love with an intern from the hospital who stops by the bar late in the evening," makes an appearance in *The Lover*.

A marvelous comment on my dual identity, or masks, turned up in a review of *Christian* that appeared in *The Review of Books and Religion*. The writer said, "It occurred to me that this work graphically portrays an author of such range in character that if he appeared in my living room, I would not know whether to serve him tea from Limoges china or beer from a can." *Which* Malcolm Boyd? I wanted to tell the writer that I would prefer the tea from Limoges china up to, say, 6:00 P.M. After that, a martini of Bombay gin with a twist. However, in all fairness to the reviewer, I should say that there are nights when I do drink beer from a can when visiting a gay leather bar.

I became accustomed to being called "controversial" in the first paragraph of virtually any print interview or the introduction of any television show. I agree with what Brooks Atkinson had to say about the use of the word: "The cowardly phrase 'controversial person' has become the permanent residue of McCarthyism; it slyly denigrates people who have independent ideas." I never claimed immunity from having independent ideas.

A Leap of Faith

After announcing publicly that I am gay, I received scores of remarkable letters—honest, incredibly touching, a few heartbreakingly sad, many joyful and profoundly hopeful—from gays and nongays all over America.

Not all the letters were warm and supportive. A few were gross insults, and, interestingly, these were generally unsigned. "Some time ago you proved your mental derangement by declaring yourself an admitted homosexual," said one anonymous letter. "May God have mercy on your soul. The atheistic, communistic propaganda machine has used you well. Ancient God-fearing *Jews* punished homosexuality by death. Today the atheistic, communistic *Jew* condones it. This latter type of *Jew* is spread across our land like a foul, rotten disease that must be wiped out. It's not too late, Malcolm. Repent." Another writer said, "Your [*sic*] just a cocksucking atheist that is out to ruin our country. I think your another communist." One commented, "You should *never* use the word gay with the same breath with the Lord. He *hates* gay." And another: "The Jesus in me loves you. But as I watched you on the TV set, I wept openly that the sweet and tender Jesus that I love so much would be distorted and misrepresented. I ask you to return to the God of Abraham, Isaac and me. All Glory to Jesus."

The letters represented polarized views in America concerning gayness. Most of the antigay letters I received quoted over and over the same few scriptural passages (Leviticus, Sodom and Gomorrah, Paulist texts) that traditionally have been used to condemn homosexuality but recently have been interpreted quite differently by a number of biblical scholars.

I am instructed by the words of Father Gerard S. Sloyan, biblical scholar and New Testament editor of the New American Bible. He wrote, "The Christian churches must resist with all their strength the literalist spirit that is destructive of the Bible. . . . Otherwise, this instrument of God's revelation will serve as a club to destroy imagined enemies rather than a fire to purge and a balm to heal. The Scriptures are meant to allay madness, not to induce it."

God is revealed in Holy Scripture, tradition, and reason. God's revelation surely continues in our present world in the forward thrust of life that includes one's own unfolding experience of living under the guidance of the Holy Spirit. Surely full knowledge of God cannot be consigned simplistically to particular interpretations of particular pages of the Bible, the doctrines of an existing church, or the insights of a new movement.

What is God's view of homosexuality? God accepts sex. God created it. God is concerned whenever sex with another person is exploitative, unloving, or undertaken for purely selfish reasons and with absolute indifference to another person's feelings and needs. God's concern is directed equally, I believe, toward gays and nongays.

I do not argue for license instead of freedom. License is an old and tried form of slavery to self. Freedom is dependent on bending one's own self-will to accept responsibility for other people. "Sexual liberation," a hardy perennial, is a healthy and holy aspect of the human adventure. Yet when it moves too far into mere rebellion and loses its spontaneity and joy in jaded calisthenics and competitive performance, it needs to be recalled (or moved forward) to a certain innocence that is unashamed of love.

Sexual conformity has been propagated by rote. The sexlessness of Jesus has been taught by the church. "Jesus is never painted in a muscular way," someone told me in a forthright and disarming way. "This seems to be on the grounds that he would be too sexual. But Jesus was a carpenter. Go out to a building site and look at a carpenter. They are strong and brown from the sun. They are healthy. They sweat. They feel the wood, the sawdust, the earth. They are alive. Jesus is always depicted on the cross wearing a loincloth. But he had every bit of standard equipment that we all have. He was a real person. Jesus of the flowing pastel robes, the sweet red mouth, and the perfect complexion, with the sea of Galilee behind you—you aren't real. At least you aren't real enough for me. I want a Jesus I can talk to, tell my secrets to, yes, even tell my jokes to. I need a real Jesus, not some plastic statue that tells me *no* all the time."

This reminds me of the extraordinary furor that greeted my quite factual comment on television a few years ago when I said, "Jesus had a penis."

More recently confronted by an intransigent fundamentalism that denied God's love to gay people, I recalled the

American Book and Bible House's publication in 1900 of a work entitled *The Negro a Beast*. It argued from a self-serving interpretation of Holy Scripture that a black person is not a descendant of Adam and Eve but is simply a beast without a soul. Blacks were taught that their enslavement was because they were cursed by God. This heresy, this blasphemy, was fixed in the minds of countless churchgoing white people. This happened *on the basis* of interpretation of the Bible. Millions of Jews have been killed *on the basis* of interpretation of the Bible.

I see danger and horror in the twisting of God's word to excuse, even encourage, torture and killing, repression of differences, and the harsh demands of authoritarianism.

As a person caught up in controversy surrounding the gay question, I perceive that I am somehow strangely closer to the way of the cross than ever before in my life. When I first entered a seminary in 1951, I believed that I was taking a leap of faith. I relinquished a career, with its accouterments of security and prestige, to follow Jesus Christ. But soon the assurance and ease of an insulated ecclesiastical existence were unmistakably felt. There was really little gospel risk at all. Gut human issues were shunted aside in favor of politics concerning who would be elected a bishop, warfare over power and personalities within a local church, raising money for a new parish building, and which revision of a prayer book to support.

Even though I was labeled as "controversial," my security was intact. But suddenly, upon announcing that I was gay, I knew that in a strange sense I had lost my life. "You would narrow your comprehension of the gospel if, because you feared to lose your life, you would keep it yourself," states the Rule of Taizé. "*If the grain does not die, you* cannot hope to see your person open up in the fullness of the Christian life. . . . Like Abraham, you can advance in this way only by faith and not by sight, being assured always that he who will have lost his life on account of Christ will find it."

Old truth. Hard truth. Redeeming truth. Long familiar with it, I had often shied away from its hard illumination. Now caught in events quite beyond my understanding or ability to cope with them, was I being compelled in an unimaginable bit of irony (for I was also under condemnation) to walk along the way of the cross *in this way?* The answer was utterly beyond my comprehension. But I knew that in the deepest recesses of my soul I had chosen life, with its unpredictable valleys and mountains, its tests and glories, over the plastic death of security, withdrawal, monochrome rigidity, and the refusal to risk. What this foretold for me, I had no way of knowing.

I was grateful, however, for the deepening of life and commitment to Christ. Many people, including myself, had long placed immediate career priorities and the realization of future goals ahead of discovering the true meaning of living. Looking around me, I saw people who had become satiated with affluence and the boring death of what is euphemistically called the good life. Now I had at least been granted a reprieve from such things.

Wholeness

CHAPTER SIX

I was asked by *Psychology Today* to write a review of Sam Keen's book *Beginnings Without End*. I found this question in the book: "How to combine private satisfaction and public dis-ease, the contentment with which the body must be nourished with the prophetic outrage which is the only appropriate reaction to the public world we have created through technology?" Keen had posed precisely the right question *for me*. By doing so, he caused the focus with which I looked at my life to shift. I realized that I had long reacted to public dis-ease with a certain prophetic outrage, but had utterly failed to nourish my body with contentment or achieve a modicum of private satisfaction. I had tragically settled for being a symbol, an image, and a thing instead of an integrated person.

This, in turn, called into question everything that I had done. It indicated a false quality in my whole life. For it meant that I had paternalistically sought to help others—as an escape of sorts?—even while I was unable or unwilling to confront and help myself. Clearly my work was cut out for me. I had to find, and accept, the wholeness that had eluded me.

Most of my life I had been pulled in opposi̇ by what I believed were the needs of the body and the soul. I interpreted the former as being related gayness and generally repressed them. I asked, did two ̇ ferent people dwell inside me, occupying my flesh and bones? Must I invariably be torn between two competing forces? Occasionally when I lapsed in my harsh resolve and met the needs of my body, I felt somewhat depraved and quite guilty.

Now I could see clearly that the needs and demands of the body and the soul constantly overlap in my being. They cannot be treated as if they were competitors, polarized from one another, with one labeled "good" and the other "bad." Ever so gradually, I moved from self-identification as "homosexual" to "gay." As I did so, I also moved out of isolation into relationship—finally, into community. I learned increasingly that I must share the fullness of my humanity, as well as that part of it that is gayness. But achieving a sense of self-worth as a gay person had to precede sharing it.

What had I gained? My soul perhaps. I was surely born again.

My vision of victory had long been a mangled body on a cross covered with flies. In other words, I did not measure real success in terms of public acceptance, prestige, or affluence. Christ's cross was my symbol of success. At the depths of my being I knew that God does not envisage success or failure according to the measurements of a competitive human society. Jesus' humble birth in a manger, stripped of its flip sentimentality, makes the same profound statement about this as does the cross.

Self-worth is a gift of God. This fact gradually permeated my consciousness. I did not have to earn it; I had only to accept it with gratitude. As I relaxed in this new consciousness, I was able to see that my former feeling of inadequacy as a gay person had made me be defensive. This, in turn, had made me rationalize that I was superior to other people, especially those whom I wished to help. Do you understand? It had sadly been necessary for me to feel superior in order to justify my existence, which I believed was inferior.

Now I was liberated from such a heretical delusion. A new phase of my life began. In contrast to earlier days when I attended a meeting or conference as a "star" guest speaker— arriving late and departing early, keeping human interaction to a minimum—now I arrived early, departed late, and enjoyed listening to other people more than speaking to them. I no longer had a "star" role to play or maintain. Everyone else knew the flesh, bones, and spirit that make up my life. Pretense would be absurd and pointless. I found this a marvelously freeing experience.

When I stood in front of people to speak, or sat before television cameras waiting to film an interview, I no longer had a desired or needed role to project. My naked face, thoughts, and feelings were acceptable. Why? Because I knew that God accepted me; I did, too; I was willing and able to throw myself on the mercy of other people to make the same decision if they wished.

A part of my nakedness is the way that I respond emotionally in public. I am a Zorba person who must sometimes dance or shed quick tears. I found support for the latter from Christopher Isherwood in *Christopher and His Kind:* "A grown man who can shed tears without embarrassment is like a yogi who has learned to expel toxic matter from his body by

consciously speeding up the peristaltic rhythm. He can elim-
inate many of life's poisons."

I want to be spared any prescribed role and all stereotyped nonsense that would even remotely limit the full range
of my humanity. This is why I find a celebrity role is finally
so utterly banal. The celebrity mask is the stupidest, most
mocking one of all. The essential character of a person is
what matters, not an image whose value can fluctuate like
a shaky stock market or mercurial Gallup poll. Our society
tends to cut off a middle ground from creative people. One
must be labeled either a superstar or a failure. Nonsense.
Sheer rubbish. If you are secure as a person and free of fool-
ish image requirements, you can eschew such dehumaniz-
ing categories. You are free to be a person, yourself.

As I met more and more gays in various parts of America, I was astonished to find that a really large number of
them are liberated people who do not give a tinker's damn
about playing public roles. They show a high degree of
self-acceptance. This is especially true of a new breed of
young gays. Their profound sense of self-worth, buoyed
by the openness of their lives outside a claustrophobic closet,
gives them an exuberant experience of personal fulfillment,
shared community, and the common goal of participating
in human liberation. Yet the new breed of gays includes
older people, too. An older gay couple whom I met in
Chicago, and another in San Francisco, were every bit as liberated as any young turks I knew. Large segments of the
public, totally out of touch with gay experiences, might
still be hung up on cliché homosexual stereotypes. However,
I found the reality and hope of the gay situation in radically new life-styles informed by confidence, joy, and openness.

In *The Sexual Outlaw,* John Rechy asks, "But are homosexuals discovering their particular *and varied* beauty? From that of the transvestite to that of the bodybuilder? The young to the old? The effeminate to the masculine? The athletic to the intellectual?" Rechy observes, "Gays must be allowed variations." I certainly agree.

My own wholeness depended on several related factors. I had made a clear decision to survive by placing a life of high energy over a slow death. This meant that I risked everything to do it. I asserted myself and my right to live. I adamantly did this in the face of censure, misunderstanding, social embarrassment, and danger. I willed to die and be born again. I cast my lot with open truth. This decision, and how I defined the meaning of truth, would henceforth permeate every part of my life. I unequivocally moved into a full awareness and celebration of gay life, yet refused to reside in a ghetto.

Howard Brown said at the poignant conclusion of *Familiar Faces, Hidden Lives* that, in his opinion, it will take the rest of this century for society to rid itself of its homosexual prejudice. "A new generation of homosexual men and women will have to grow up secure in their identity, knowing from the start that gay people can be happy, loving, and of value to society. And a new generation of straight men and women will have to grow up never having doubted that gay people are people." I agree that it seems entirely possible that happier days for gay people lie ahead.

However, ominous signs point toward a rise of authoritarianism. There is an increased use of torture by many governments. One finds numerous harsh demands for conformity. A constant threat is directed against the climate of

free inquiry and free speech in which gay liberation has successfully been advanced in recent years. Significant setbacks
range from troglodytic U.S. Supreme Court negativism to intransigent religiosity. For example, the Reverend Albert
Outler, a theologian, told a conference of United Meth-
odists in the summer of 1976 that extending a welcome to
"all persons, regardless of sexual orientation," would further
a "drift into decadence." He said, "We're being asked here
and now to condone homosexuality. This is wrong, unwise,
and a foolproof recipe for disaster in the church and society." A prominent New York columnist noted that homosexuality is a sin and not a crime and that to practice it is to
break moral codes but no constitutional laws. So, the place
of gays remained ambiguous and undefined in American life.

This is why I am appalled by the naive pursuit of individual
pleasure by many gays and lesbians, who fail to see the necessity of social organization and the development of actual,
unified, muscled gay power. This is a moment when gays and
lesbians can be openly expressive and political. What a tragedy
if the moment is casually wasted, and the horror of repression and persecution looms ahead. Now is a time for gays and
lesbians to be political. Harvey Cox said in *The Feast of Fools,*
"Celebration without politics becomes effete and empty.
Politics without celebration becomes mean and small. The
festive spirit knows how to toast the future, drink the wine,
and break the cup. They all belong together."

A sense of prophetic outrage, then, truly belongs with
personal contentment in a contemporary gay life-style that
is committed to social justice as well as individual growth.
Three street liturgies in the late sixties and early seventies
stand out vividly in my memory as honest expressions of
protest against social wrongs.

Snow fell softly in the late afternoon of December 21, 1969, as a group of us huddled together on a frozen New York City street corner close by the Tombs, the city jail. We protested the fact that twenty-two Black Panthers were held prisoner inside. Harvey Cox led us in the exorcism: "Out, demons, out!" I was the preacher. "In four days it will be Christmas," I said. "We cannot bask in an affluent caricature of Christmas while our brethren are denied their humanity and tortured in spirit. America, be gracious and not cruel; remain open to the cries of the hungry, the deprived, the imprisoned. Do not be deaf to those who have been deeply hurt in this land. Share the greatest bounty in the history of the world. Do not hoard goodness so that it becomes perverted and monstrous evil. America, foster life instead of death. Raise up people instead of destroying people. Do not ask us to worship you instead of God."

The other two liturgies were Peace Masses inside the Pentagon. Each led to our arrest. In one of them, I was the celebrant. Bread and wine for the service were placed on the cement floor; incense filled the air; bright eucharistic vestments were situated directly next to military uniforms. The Mass was interrupted by police who claimed there was undue noise.

In the other Peace Mass, I was designated to preach the sermon. A policeman with a bullhorn conducted an antiphonal and certainly unrehearsed dialogue with me—he tumbling out the words, "You are under arrest," I uttering a contrapuntal phrase, "If the salt has lost its taste, how shall its saltiness be restored?" On the bus taking us to jail for "disturbing the peace," we sang. Later we completed the interrupted Mass in the basement of a Washington church. When the driver of the police bus joined us in our catacomb, it seemed uncannily a bit like the early days of Christianity.

The need for expressions of prophetic outrage remains strong in American society. All human wrongs and examples of neglect are linked. The problem of the treatment of elderly people cannot be separated from the gay problem, the racial problem, women's rights, AIDS, the condition of the poor, the environmental crisis, or any other pressing social need concerning people's survival and well-being. Any myopic view that focuses on one problem while refusing to see related ones is doomed to ultimate failure.

My mother wrote to me recently about the particular plight of older people.

> The problem of the aged is terrible. People don't seem to care. They shunt the elderly into rest homes, where many practically rot and die—and welcome death, I suppose.
>
> One elderly lady, whom I had known since my college days, was the mother of a friend of mine. My friend and her husband had an extra bedroom for the mother, and no financial problems. However, the daughter had her mother picked up in a wagon and taken to the county home.
>
> I visited her there. She was in a bed with a light overhead day and night that bothered her eyes so much that she had to wear an eyeshield all the time. She used to read a great deal, but now she could not do so at all. Finally she fell out of bed and broke her hip. Then she was taken to the hospital, where she died alone. I have wondered if she threw herself out of that bed.
>
> The children of the elderly don't seem to realize that someday they will be faced with the same problems. I am

reminded of a story that my mother used to tell. An old man lived in a shack in back of the house where his son's family resided. On one very cold night the son carried out an extra blanket for his father's bed. His father took a pair of scissors and cut the blanket down the middle. The son said, "Father, why are you cutting the blanket?" The father replied, "I'm cutting it for you, so someday when you're put out of your home, you'll have a blanket."

This story is wise and prophetic. It has relevance for all sorts and conditions of people, not only the elderly. There needs to be infinitely more sharing in our society—a blanket, food, money, civil rights, a vision of hope, compassion, and justice.

Gays and nongays alike need to work together for the increase of the quality of life, liberty, and the pursuit of happiness. This is not a moment when one dares to pull back into the solitariness of one's self-concern or individual growth. Concern for self must be balanced with steady social action.

The fact is, however, that many people are simply unwilling to recognize as legitimate the kind of human difference represented by gayness or to grant such difference any visibility or equal rights. Others who do not hold such an extreme view nevertheless are frightened by stereotypes of gayness and lack even the beginnings of an understanding of gay people.

Closet has become a universal code word in contemporary language. At first it referred to closet gays, who hid from public revelation of their identity, choosing to keep secret their sexual orientation and life-style. But soon one began to read about closet drinkers, closet sexists, closet liberals, and a whole gamut of other categories of closet people.

A significant contribution gay people can offer is the awareness that virtually everybody occupies some kind of closet. Everybody knows what it means to hide and experience loneliness, refusing or being unable to share and explain deep feelings and truths.

In this connection, I recall how deeply hurt I was nearly two decades ago when my relationship with another gay man broke into a million pieces. We had long hidden in closets from one another, known loneliness in our mutuality, and been unable to share deep feelings and hard truths. Our good-bye was desperately joyless and mutually mean. Recently I wrote him a letter—which represented at least an intense desire to step outside a closet—yet I did not mail it. Here is the letter, which now no longer rests inside a closet.

5:00 P.M.

Dear N.:

Please forgive the obvious and certainly rude intrusion this letter represents. I realize we aren't speaking, haven't "spoken" for fifteen years; by any accepted rules of conduct, this should extend to writing. Am I opening up old wounds that had healed? If so, I apologize. You see, my wounds never happened to heal.

What happened? Did we hold implausible and inhuman mutual expectations concerning one another that could not be met? Were there a monumental clash and critical wounding of egos? Or was it more: a clear summing up of realities in both of our lives and then an obdurate refusal of them?

In any event, there was a refusal, apparently on both of our parts, to remain in any kind of relationship. Each of us touted up provocations for being hurt, numerical points emphasizing the other's lack of goodness, and logical reasons why we ought not be friends. Then we acted logically.

How are you? I've heard various rumors about where you have been and what you have done, but would appreciate a firsthand report. Have you been happy? Do you feel your life is fulfilled? What's new?

Looking back, I've got my own theories about what happened between us. I believe that you constructed an ideal image of me and then proceeded to relate to it. You did this because it seemed so neatly possible for the ideal image to meet what you considered your needs. I realize that I had no idea what your actual needs were. But I thought that I knew them. To further complicate the picture, I assumed that I was meeting them. It was inside this idyllic paradise that all hell broke loose. Volcanoes erupted. Hot lava poured down mountain slopes, engulfing whole villages. Fires raged. The sky was filled with forbidding spirals of dense smoke.

Damn it, why couldn't we talk to one another? If we had tried, I guess we might have come close to killing each other off. We had managed, without being aware of it, to touch the rawest of nerves. There must previously have been love between us because now the hate seemed so strong. Or could it have been the fury of realizing, in a coherent moment, that we had invested so much blood and emotion in an idyllic farce? When it broke wide open, we felt, each of us, a stranger in a forbidding world of terror and hurt.

Humpty Dumpty gets glued together every hour, on the hour. So there are surely no stray pieces of our brokenness lying on the ground to be placed on a very private shelf or examined for clues concerning the murder. Are you guilty of it? Am I? It seems an absurdly academic question, the matter of guilt. The murder itself is a fact of life, to be lived with. We have both done so for quite a long time.

Not to be vulgar (at least by intention), but simply to look at ourselves in the present givenness of some perspective: Have you any idea how really, grimly hurt I was? (Were you, too?) I have no demands that I wish to make upon you now. I only wonder if you are well. I hope so.

Love,
Malcolm

The imagery of the closet makes a compelling statement about the ways that we humans imprison ourselves, cutting off communication with others.

Vittorio de Sica's classic film *Umberto D* concerns an old man living in Italy, a young woman who is pregnant but does not know which of two lovers is her baby's father, and a dog that is the old man's beloved companion. De Sica described the meaning of the film: "It seeks to put on the screen the drama of man's inability to communicate. When everything is at a dead end, when there is no more hope of getting help from anybody, it is just then that Umberto could have found a way out. By taking the girl out of this house, being a father to her. Two or three, together might solve their problems." The point of de Sica's film is that these people did not solve their problems because they remained locked inside solitary closets.

In Jean Paul Sartre's *No Exit,* someone cries out, "Hell is other people!"; that is one concept of hell. But the philosopher and playwright Gabriel Marcel discovered a deeper truth: "There is only one suffering: to be alone." To be locked inside a closet of one's devising or hard choice is to experience an agony of modern mass life, what it is like to be a solitary individual in a lonely crowd.

Some individuals choose to be solitary and reclusive, far away from a lonely crowd. I discovered a most poignant example of this on an August afternoon in 1975 when I abruptly entered the celebrated closet of Mary Pickford.

Occasional news stories had increasingly raised questions, some sensational ones, about her reclusive existence of recent years on her estate in California. What was the state of her mental and physical health? What were her own wishes concerning her existence? She had not been seen by the public. (The one exception, which followed my visit, was a brief filmed interview on an Academy Award telecast. After that the curtain fell again.)

Only a few intimates had any contact with her. Now she was in her eighties. I had not seen Mary for many years. But then Esther Helm, her private secretary, telephoned me to convey Miss Pickford's invitation to pay her a visit. I was absolutely surprised and delighted at the prospect of seeing her. The approaching meeting with Mary was particularly touching for me because I had been close to her years before.

I arrived at Pickfair at 1:30 P.M. A maid admitted me and asked me to wait. I wandered through the silent and empty downstairs rooms. Mary's portrait hung over the living-room grate. A single photograph of Elsie de Wolfe, Lady Mendl—inscribed "To a Beloved! Elsie, 1935"—stood on a table. Lady Mendl, one of the most elegant women in modern history, wore a tiara. Her gown with its slim shoulder straps was a classic evocation of a golden era. Her face, timeless as Nefertiti's, conjured up images of high elegance and unrestricted privilege. Photographs of other famed Pickfair guests in the past, Queen Marie of Romania and the Mountbattens of the English court, occupied walls of other rooms. I walked through the still-life dining room, which had once been as sought-after a place for an invitation as the White House. In the hallway hung another portrait of Mary with her famous golden curls. Silence.

Miss Helm came down and told me that I could go upstairs now to see Mary. When I entered the room, I saw Mary stretched out on a bed. Her nurse left us alone. Mary's emotion was unrestrained. She placed her tiny, frail hands around my body, hugging me for a long time. During the hour of our conversation, she held both my hands tightly in hers, except when she traced the lines of my face with her fingers. We called one another "sweetheart" and "dear." She called me her "spiritual son" and held my face closely next to hers for a long time. She spoke of forgiveness, and God, and the great pain she had suffered. She said her veined hands were like those of a monkey, but I said my hairy hands were much more so. We laughed and reminisced.

I recalled a happier time with Mary in 1954, while I was a student at the seminary in Berkeley. Mary visited San Francisco as cochairperson with Mrs. Dwight D. Eisenhower of a savings bond campaign. Mary astonished media reporters who sought to patronize her as an "aging actress" only to discover quickly that she remained a scene stealer without shame, far outpacing everyone else in making an expert use of the media.

At nights, when she had finished her official duties, we ate Italian dinners with hot buttered garlic bread. Mary wore her diamonds even while taking a cable-car ride with me.

One night Mary kindly accepted an invitation offered at my behest to dine at the seminary. After dinner she addressed the future clerics. Her traditional image of "men of God" was on a collision course with the self-image of new-breed clergy. The occasion proved to be an embarrassment to all concerned. My peer group's negative reactions to her visit were undisguised.

The next morning Mary sent red roses to be placed on the altar of the seminary chapel. The lovely flowers, alongside a heavy metal cross, conjured up strange feelings inside the seminary community. Guilt came first, because a certain insider community bitchiness had acknowledgedly been the spontaneous response to Mary's bad performance. Irritation followed. It was directed again at Mary, the interloper Hollywood personage who had seemingly created the unsavory situation in the first place and hence was allegedly the reason for everyone's needing to feel guilt. Finally the church-trained concept of penance took precedence over judging a guest. So the seminary community made at least an implicit statement of *mea culpa*. This found expression in fresh (and, I knew, enjoyed) guilt.

Now, talking to Mary in her bedroom at Pickfair, my hands held hers. Tears rolled down her face. She pointed to her father's and mother's photographs that hung on the wall. "Papa died when I was four, but I love him just as much as Mama," she said. A depiction of Jesus in the Greek Orthodox style hung over her bedroom fireplace. I saw the person of Mary, not the persona. She was warm and gracious, the Mary whose life was so intertwined at past moments with my own. She asked if I wanted a servant to bring me a sandwich and a drink. I said no, thanks.

I looked closely into Mary's face. I was in the presence of someone who had once been called the world's most celebrated and beautiful woman. But beauty changes, celebrity dims, applause ceases. Mary had probably autographed thousands of photographs during her career; yet after I departed I sent her a smiling, sunny, happy photograph of myself to be placed on a table near her bed as a reminder simply of a friend who reached out in tenderness and love and did not forget her. I wrote "To Mary—Love" and signed my name.

The importance I am giving to the meeting with Mary Pickford says a great deal more about me, including my attitude toward worldly acclaim, than it does about her.

While I recognize the glamour of celebrity, I also see the fickle transitoriness and absurd quality of it. To take oneself *that* seriously, suspect that the world revolves in a dizzying orbit around oneself, forget the singular brevity of warm acclaim as well as of life itself—this is absurd.

I believe this realization helped me to come out of my closet as a gay person and hopefully out of other closets in my life as well. Time is so short. It is pure tragedy, in my opinion, to hide behind a mask, sacrifice one's well-being to the idol of a desired image, deliberately waste the essence of creativity because of fearful insecurity, or permit vital energy to be lost as a result of not making a positive decision. So, I decided while there was still time that I wish to harbor death no longer in my days on earth. I will restrict the enjoyment of tragedy to the theater. I choose life.

After I left Mary, I swam in the kidney-shaped pool in the garden of Pickfair. The perfectly maintained great lawn sloped downward toward the pool. It was surrounded by a lush garden of flowers. A massive pine tree loomed overhead. Butterflies played amid the flowers. There was no sound but the wind rustling leaves and birds singing.

Why, I wondered, had Mary chosen her reclusive closet so many years ago, turning her back on the action and risks of life with other people? Hers was surely the oddest of closets, a luxurious one inhabited by ghosts and sadness. I was grateful that she had briefly shared it with me. But I did not like her closet, basically because I still loved her as a friend and wanted liberation and joy for the woman named Mary Pickford.

So, I learned, closets come in all different sizes and colors. The rich and poor, the unknown and famous, occupy them alike. There are many vastly different kinds of closets for human beings who wear an army of masks.

Racial separation, or any form of human apartheid, means the existence of separate closets in which people dwell, hidden from each other, mere images going through the motions of communicating. A black friend of mine found himself in a closet racial experience during the 1967 race riot in Detroit: "Old women sat on ghetto street curbs, moaning and laughing hysterically. Everything was chaos—fires raging, guns going off. National Guardsmen running, looted stores. I found an unbroken bottle of gin outside a torn-up liquor store. I poured the gin in an empty beer can and sipped it slowly as I walked twenty, thirty blocks. A white soldier with a gun pushed me hard and said, 'You can't walk here, you black son of a bitch.' 'Don't *touch* me, you goddamn white devil,' I told him. 'It's Whitey we're killing today.' He just stood there looking dazed. I kept walking, sipping the gin."

A student described another kind of closet, a religious one: "Sunday after Sunday, I heard a creed that I couldn't understand. What's worse, I said it. I and everyone else said the Lord's Prayer automatically, you know, just like ordering a beer or like an answer to a call from my mother. Church was a place where Jonah really got swallowed by a whale and the Red Sea parted, and the youth of America was called degenerate, lazy, loud, oversexed, having no sense of values, forethought, hindsight, or shined shoes. I heard people tell me that the Bible says the blacks are the descendants of Cain and will forever bear a cursed scar. We talked about how the sinful Catholics were out to steal from the Latin Americans, and how we would save the Buddhists from the eternal fire. All the good folks in church would nod their heads in the appropriate directions and go right on thinking about that horse that didn't come in, or that ulcer, or that busted television set."

The young man, locked inside his churchly closet experience, did not communicate his feelings to other people in the church. He stopped attending. Others who were there did not communicate to him how they felt. They remained locked inside their closets and saw him depart from their midst without a word.

My two-month odyssey through America in the fall of 1976 helped me to understand how various people struggle courageously to come out of their own closets and realistically grapple with life, sometimes triumphantly.

In Toronto I met a woman who had known the closet experience of being a woman in a male-dominated church structure: "I knew I wanted to be a priest. I also knew the necessity of women's roles to influence a man—either to be seductive or else play daddy's little girl to win points. I sat in front of the bishop and said, 'I want to be ordained.' He said, 'You know that's impossible.' I walked out feeling equal. I appropriated the parent role. I was able to make the claim within myself. That was the moment when I really said, 'I am worthy.' I no longer had to play games to win the goodwill of male authority figures. I want to test myself in cosexual structures. I'm not going to be a castrated male or a desexed woman. People are troubled by menstrual blood. There is a kind of primitive resistance. People respond to 'Father' and what it means to be paternal. People's reaction to 'Mother' is different. There is an anxiety that their view of God will be changed."

In Portland, Oregon, I met someone who worked with many elderly women and men and perceived the existence of closets where these people were labeled and confined. He opened up these closet doors for them: "I don't believe in 'senior citizen centers'—'senior citizens.' Older people need to be looked upon as human beings. We try to do this and also meet their housing needs. We try to offer them choices. We take them to different places. We check ventilation, how many steps they'll have to climb, if the elevator door is hard to open. But the best is one-to-one relationships. Training is trying to understand the hurt, the real embarrassment."

In San Francisco I met a man who let religion and the arts come out of their separate closets and meet in a creative, lively way. We chatted inside a church that had been converted into a theater and coffeehouse. An espresso machine stood on the old wooden altar in the basement coffeehouse. Upstairs the theater ticket booth was the former church pulpit. "There was always an awareness that the church and the arts were aligned," he said. "They somehow have a similar kind of mission but use a different language."

In Chicago I met a nun who had moved outside the closet of personal piety into the arena of people's needs. She spoke of the work that engaged her time and energies: "Hunger is an area of concentration for us. It's an uphill battle. Legislative issues are not popular. But if you keep at national health insurance and food stamps, year after year, you get closer. It's better to get church people involved in other people's needs than intellectualizing about it."

In southern California I met a young minister who, with the rest of the people in his church, had come out of many personal closets and joined in a community that tried to heal its own members and serve the needs of other people. "Most people here have done EST, TM, slept with everybody, been involved in this movement or that one, and they want some way of putting it together. The community we have is disenfranchised. We have to empower it. Part of this is for people to feel power in their own lives. Our theater company is here because they do improvisation. That's the way we have to play our lives. We can't depend on structures. Outside of a few game rules, we have to wing it. Improvisation is necessarily built on trust."

In Houston I met a teacher who spoke candidly about closets in a medical school and how certain students came to a deep religious sense in grappling with taboos that they considered part of their religion: "Anatomy comes early in medical school. Students have to deal with naked bodies, shave off hair, cut off flesh. But ours is a puritan culture. That's a taboo. Death is also a taboo, for we deny our mortality. So students are thrust into both taboos immediately. Their superficial knowledge of religion tells them this violates their religion. But we say, 'No, it does not.' So they come curiously to the very depths of religion."

The mystery of being gay puzzles and astonishes me. Why are there gays? What does it mean to be the Jew, the black, the gay, someone who must suffer in a particular way within the "normal majority" culture? What, if any, unique mission or vocation is involved in this? One is compelled to ask such questions when one is different and belongs to such a sharply defined minority.

Gay used to stand for pretense and patterned choreography, playing prescribed roles and wearing masks. "Make it gay" was the watchword. It meant "put on the ritz," "keep the act going," "don't let down your guard," "keep on smiling"—especially to conceal your sadness.

But there has been a change. Gay now means a new honesty. Where it used to signify wearing a mask, now it is a call to take off the masks. Its definition has shifted from form to content, sheer style to reality.

So, gay has something of universal meaning to say to everybody. Take off the masks of repressed anger, self-pity, sexual deceit, hypocrisy, social exploitation, and spiritual arrogance. Let communication be an event that involves people, not a charade of puppets. Be yourself. Relate to other selves without inhibition and pretense. Help others to be themselves, too.

The journey toward self-honesty includes the study of one's myths. Everybody has them. So do you and I. Since we invariably create many of our personal myths, it should not be extraordinarily difficult for us to perceive them honestly.

Also, most of us have painstakingly constructed our own masks, the ones that we wear and change ritualistically as we move from one situation to another, from this relationship to that. To take off the masks is to stop the ritual for its own sake and let life replace it.

What happens to a person whose mask has been shed? Speaking for myself, I feel better than ever before. I am incredibly energized. I acknowledge the mystery of my creation and my own mission within it. The reality of myself, as a person created in God's image, is openly shared for the first time. I am grateful that I did not go to the grave without sharing it happily. My closet door is unhinged. Light and air are flooding into that claustrophobic dungeon cell in which I spent more than fifty years of my life.

Beyond all expectation, I have discovered release and freedom, joy and love. Isn't the purpose of our lives to develop and evolve with every breath we take, in every second we live? I have been able to risk everything, and this at an age when many people begin to settle in for their end.

With great zest I celebrate life. I have countless friends. I am filled with joy and gratitude. I love. I am evolving as a person. How could I possibly ask for anything more?

I have learned that a mask is a lie, that it obscures deep truths, that it gets in the way of life. The time has come to take off the masks.

Epilogue

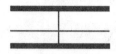

A wedding party surrounded the bride and groom in a grove of redwood trees. It was a spring day in the mid 1980s at Big Sur on the California coast. The lively service combined song, dance, and readings. People wore happy smiles. I found it a warm, touching experience.

I had attended heterosexual wedding ceremonies all my life, wished joy and godspeed to the newlyweds, and sincerely supported them in their new commitments. However, I wondered, was there ever going to be a place for me as a gay man to find a similar kind of support in a relationship? Could I ever expect to look at such happy smiles and greet a ritual of absolute openness blessing my covenant with a man whom I love?

In the midst of the celebratory scene at Big Sur I resolved to quit being an outsider to happiness. Enough of pain, neurosis, and feeling deprived! The next week I formally proposed to my lover, Mark Thompson, and offered him a ring. He accepted. Shortly thereafter we settled into our home, becoming a new couple on our city block. As I write this, we are in our eighth year as partners.

A funny 1987 Valentine's Day listing of well-known gay and lesbian pairings turned up this quip: "Made in Heaven:

David and Jonathan, Mark Thompson and Malcolm Boyd, Cardinal Newman and Brother Ambrose." When writer Steve Abbott interviewed Mark and me that year for the *San Francisco Sentinel,* he asked about our relationship. "I see it as a holy voyage, fraught with mystery," I said. "That's a good way of putting it," Mark agreed. "A holy voyage full of mystery and delight."

I told the interviewer, "I think it's important to start over in life several times, to open yourself up to new directions. We don't have forever; we have to live now." I've come to understand this during the thirteen years since I wrote *Take Off the Masks.* My life has changed in extraordinary ways. At moments it seems I am hardly the same person. One reason is that I have finally found personal happiness and well-being. But I was startled not long ago when someone remarked, "I'm sorry you're happy, if you are. Your writing meant so much to me when you suffered."

Who knows who suffers? Pain is a part of life. I am sharply reminded of this due to the fact that Mark has the AIDS virus and is HIV positive. Yet we manage to live successfully with this reality day by day, as so many others do. We experience joy and transformation in being thankful for the new day at hand, living it to the fullest.

I am a man of the city, raised in Manhattan, intimately at home in the labyrinths of New York and Los Angeles. Mark, raised in Carmel, is at home with nature and the elements. So he has introduced me to Big Sur, Yosemite, the Mexican coast, and Hawaii. When we vacationed on Kauai we stayed in a rustic cottage on a deserted beach. The only sounds I heard at night were the ocean roar and, sometimes, a rooster crowing. When we hiked along the coast of Na Pali, I climbed from one rock to another. Soon we discovered a secluded beach where I walked naked in the sun, the waves breaking over my feet.

Another vacation took us outside Cancun on Mexico's Yucatán peninsula. Our thatch-roofed cabana was mere steps away from an unspoiled beach. When I walked on the soft, white sand it resembled snow. At night, with the jungle foliage only a few feet away, I encountered another, invisible world with its gods, demons, faeries, monsters, beneficent powers, and magical spirits. One afternoon a tropical storm came up suddenly. We ran along the beach while the rain drenched us, palm branches blew furiously in the wind, and clouds scattered like pieces of cotton in the sky.

Mark and I rented a Volkswagen bug and drove to the ruins of Chichén Itzá. The pyramids were fascinating, but I can't climb them as easily as I used to. There is a pervasive melancholy about Chichén Itzá; the dead Mayans seem to be active ghosts in the ruins. I wondered: What will be our North American ruins? The Empire State Building? Golden Gate Bridge? MGM? The Pentagon? Back at our cabana, I loved swimming nude in the Caribbean and taking a nap afterward beneath a palm tree, using a coconut shell for my pillow.

Mark is an editor who also writes books. *Gay Spirit: Myth and Meaning* is one. *Leatherfolk* is another. Two writers under one roof? Yes. It works out very well. We are not competitive, but like to help each other find the right word or image, tell the best story, in order to communicate.

With the start of the 1980s I began a decade of spiritual work at St. Augustine-by-the-Sea Episcopal Church in Santa Monica, where I have preached, celebrated the Eucharist, and conducted workshops. One was called "Take Off the Masks." I asked participants to make their own masks with paper and crayons; ours was a collective search for identity.

At St. Augustine's I helped create two of the first AIDS Masses in the United States. The Gay Men's Chorus sang at AIDS Mass I on May 5, 1985; I was the celebrant. Reactions were swift and positive. "I never thought the church really cared about us until now," a person with AIDS said.

A gay journalist assigned to cover the event explained his feelings at the outset: "I felt a deep rage. The church had always been an enemy. Religion had been intolerant, judgmental, unloving. Yet I realized something altogether new was happening before my eyes as well as inside myself when the Mass started. I found myself sobbing. I realized I was offered a bridge, not another closed door. There were love, and openness, and sharing."

I preached the sermon at AIDS Mass II on September 29, 1985. "Jesus was only thirty-three when he died," I said. "Around the same age as many dying of AIDS right now. . . . We're all going to die: monarchs and poets, soldiers and lawyers, bakers and balladeers. That's a given. What I'm beginning to realize is that what matters is how we live. The way we live, the quality of our lives, in this moment we have."

AIDS has become devastatingly more personal with the deaths of close friends. One of mine was Robert A. Kettelhack, an Episcopal priest. The very first time I saw Bob—and then through the years—I was struck by his resemblance to those great and beautiful men in the paintings of El Greco. Bob possessed an olive-hued, elegantly lean, classic face; liquid eyes in whose glance one caught vulnerability as well as deep strength; gentle and electric energy in his lithe body; and a warm smile that could illuminate a room.

It was hard to watch Bob's long crucifixion with AIDS. I saw him share Christ's suffering and find peace there. It reminded me of Paul's epistle to the Philippians: "All I care is to know Christ, to experience the power of his resurrection, and to share his suffering, in growing conformity with this death, if only I may finally arrive at the resurrection from the dead." I feel this is where the gospel intersects the human heart. Taking a leaf from Paul's epistle, Bob acted in growing conformity with Christ's death.

I remember when Bob was not expected to recover from a bout with pneumocystis. He found himself in a spiritual and physical wilderness experience in which he literally wrestled with death hour after hour. I thought of Jacob's wrestling with the angel: "I will not let you go until you bless me." Bob wrestled free that time, but brushed against death again and again.

Bob's courage, faith, and love informed me that the Christian faith continues to reveal itself in the lives/epistles of people like him. It isn't simply *back there* in books such as Colossians, Thessalonians, Philippians, and Corinthians. I perceived that Bob, like the apostle Paul, was consciously pressing on: gently, obdurately; tenderly, strongly. I believe Bob saw death not as an abyss but as a natural part of life itself, an unfolding new experience with God, a spiritual adventure with Christ. Bob's life partner Jack Plimpton remains a close friend of Mark's and mine.

Looking back, I remember how my coming out in 1976 had the intensity of a tidal wave in my life. I felt a sensation of liberation and being "born again." It was exuberant and sometimes overpowering. Like a voracious Marco Polo, I explored life outside myself as if it were a new continent.

I was often surprised by the fierce internalized homophobia of the gay world, a result of savage wounds sustained by relentless oppression. I was also amazed to discover the extraordinary diversity of gay and lesbian life. It is as diverse as Jewish life. A contemporary American Jew can be characterized by a tie to Judaism, Zionism, Jewish culture: all three of these, one or two, or none. The diversity of gay people is also mind-boggling, defying all attempts to make it wear a uniform.

So, an urgent question confronted me: Where did *I* fit in the gay world? I straddled two disparate entities, "gay" and "religion." They were about as compatible as oil and water. Too much pain had been inflicted on gay people by organized religion for there to be any easy truce.

Yet I was a gay priest. A profile of me appearing in *Episcopal Life* in November 1991 noted accurately that after the public revelation of my gayness, "then came exile." Mine was a rude shock, especially when books I had written were burned in an angry ritual of rejection. For several years I wandered in a strange, unfamiliar wilderness. What to do? I was greeted as if I were a leper by many former friends and associates in organized religion.

A few friends acted to save my life. Paul Moore, Jr., then the Episcopal bishop of New York, offered every kind of support, including canonical residence in his diocese. Fred Fenton, rector of St. Augustine's Church, invited me to join his parish and resolutely stood his ground after some parishioners departed angrily and canceled their financial pledges. Art Seidenbaum, editor of the *Los Angeles Times Book Review,* gave me a long list of review and other writing assignments, along with unstinting hours of wise counsel. Art was a great listener and a humanly involved man.

Other friends made all the difference in my life by being present in positive, motivational ways. I found stimulus in the hard work of being president of PEN Center U.S.A. West from 1984 to 1987 and challenge as being chaplain of the Commission on AIDS Ministry for the Episcopal Diocese of Los Angeles.

Moving openly and actively into the gay world, I decided that I wished neither to exist within a ghetto nor to be assimilated. I believe that we gay people need to retain our sharp particularity and, at the same time, occupy our place in the world. Our experience can never be described simplistically under a label of "either/or." Ours is a "both/and" destiny. Our collective journey is our common teacher. Out of this come our individual herstories and histories.

The gay and lesbian nation now occupies a newly recognizable place; gay ethnicity is studied along with that of other minorities. So gay writing, formerly a mere trickle of books, now represents a flood of titles. As a gay writer, I am publicly identified as one who emerges from a spiritual direction and frequently deals with religious themes. However, I rebel against any stereotyping of myself or my work. I am a whole being, incredibly complex and diverse, and want this always to be recognized.

The books I have written since *Take Off the Masks* reflect such genuine diversity in my life and work. *Look Back in Joy: A Celebration of Gay Lovers* is a memoir that is marked by eroticism, sensuality, and the search for love. The *Los Angeles Times* commented, "By sharing the unextraordinariness of love's long suffusion into his life, [he] has shared with us his neatest trick of all."

The *New York Times Book Review* called *Gay Priest: An Inner Journey,* which appeared in 1986, "part memoir, part meditation, part manifesto." I wrote in it, "Honesty is the primary gift that gay people can now offer to society and the church, which show such an appalling lack of it." I explained, "My theology slowly took root in my experience and consciousness as a gay man. . . . From my view, God was never the Torturer . . . God was not the Executioner, Cruel Judge, Absolute Monarch, Totalitarian Dictator, Capricious Deity. I learned to know God as the Lover."

In 1991, when I coedited *Amazing Grace: Stories of Lesbian and Gay Faith,* I wrote, "Gay and lesbian spirituality will suffer irremediably, and no doubt vanish as a serious entity on the religious horizon, if it doesn't care for the poor, homeless, suffering, and disenfranchised outside its own parameters. AIDS is leading it to a close, deep identification with the crucified and risen Christ, who calls the gay and lesbian Christian movement to the way of the cross instead of becoming yet another religious success myth."

I realize that as a writer I have provoked wrath, fought censorship, and confronted a sometimes hypocritical society with my refusal to be conventional. I feel deeply about issues and attempt to communicate how I feel. This means on occasion being willing to enter into the dark night of my soul, someone else's soul, and the soul of the world I inhabit. It's said that writers should listen to their muses. At times I've found it more demanding—and in a curious way, nurturing—to listen to my conscience.

Out of this experience comes a sense of being fully alive; creativity is linked to life. My conscience says, "This is reality. This is *you* in reality. Do this. Dance this, compose this, act this, paint this, *write* this." A writer's pact with conscience is, in my view, a commitment to life.

In his book *Gay Spirit: Myth and Meaning,* Mark Thompson defines gay people "as possessing a *luminous* quality of being, a differentness that accentuates the gifts of compassion, empathy, healing, interpretation and enabling. I see gay people as the *in-between ones:* those who can entertain irreconcilable differences, who are capable of uniting opposing forces as one; bridge builders who intuit the light and dark in all things. These people who seem to spring from between the cracks, these androgynous alchemists, have a certain and necessary function for life on this planet."

Gay spirituality and theology stem from the differentness of gay people. Theologically, it became necessary for me to look at salvation from the vantage point of a Christian man in the process of coming out as a gay man. What did I find? First, a gift of unconditional love from a loving God; second, the need to make a response of unconditional risk and openness as an act of faith.

Concrete expression of salvation in everyday life is found in interrelating, interconnecting, integrating, and becoming at one with oneself and the universe. There is an extraordinary irony in the church's claim that it wants to "save" gay people. If it does, it's essential that it change from tolerating us to affirming our being gay. Otherwise, one can only assume that it wishes to consign us to the damnation and hell of continuing to divide and compartmentalize our lives.

I told an interviewer for *Playboy* in January 1992, "The church is afraid of sex, and it's a fear of mystery, of spontaneity—almost a fear of God." God teaches us, I believe, not to be bound by previous interpretations or ideas held as valid basically because they are old. God helps us to look at situations in fresh ways; calls us to the freedom to explore, investigate, and experiment; challenges us to grow.

A role of gay people is to bring apostate churches closer to the reality of Jesus Christ. When the church states that it is the habitat of God on earth, "the Body of Christ," one recalls in stunned silence the countless ways in which the church has blatantly betrayed God, Christ, and the commandment to love. If one believes, as I do, that God is loving, what is one to make of the church when it inexplicably reveals itself to be hostile, thorny, even hating? The contradiction is bewildering. The church must honestly deal with the contradiction, draw closer to Christ, and learn anew how to love.

As a gay Christian I have received numerous letters that invoke the name of Jesus Christ and then proceed to deliver a message of utter lovelessness and hate. One of these said, "Jesus has been so hurt by the actions of the ones he loves. Those who have given in to the temptations of lust and unnatural desires of sodomy. Homosexuality has never been and will never be accepted by Jesus. He said he has sent AIDS to the world as a plague to help the people who have practiced these types of acts to 'save their souls through suffering.' I will feel sad when I read that YOU have died of AIDS, Malcolm. I really like you so much." The letter was signed "Sincerely in Jesus."

Many lesbians and gay men, in response to such manifestations of hatred and abuse in the name of Jesus Christ, have left Christianity, its dogmas, rituals, and institutions. Some embrace New Age spirituality. Others find fulfillment in Eastern religions, particularly Buddhism; the world of Jungian analysis; and an assortment of spiritual modes of expression that emerge in gay and lesbian culture. A totally unforeseen, and utterly ironical, result of this exodus is that gay people now constitute what is probably the major urban mission field for the church in North America. This mission field will be a tough nut to crack.

For decades I have observed the church's railing against "personal" sin while it too often remained mute in the face of "public" sin. The latter found focus in a wide sweep of terrible events ranging from the casual use of torture to institutionalized racism and massive forms of dehumanization. It has struck me as sinful beyond words, an affront to God. I must add that while masturbation seemed natural to me, anti-Semitism and racism never did.

The church taught that salvation was a free gift of God, bestowed by Christ's action of at-one-ment on the cross. I found that a corollary of this meant for a Christian to accept responsibility as a cocreator in the continuing act of creation. Salvation, then, was integrated into the warp and woof of the human experience. Social action became an indispensable part of a belief in salvation. *When* (Jesus asked) did we apparently not see him? When Jesus, in the guise of a needy person, was thirsty, hungry, homeless, naked, and in prison, and we did nothing to help. *When* (Jesus asked) did we apparently see him? When we responded to the human need of another person—and ministered to him in that person. For example, a "nigger," a "kike," a "dago," a "queer," a "dyke," or a "faggot."

I have encouraged the development of gay and lesbian theology and spirituality during the years since I wrote *Take Off the Masks*. Speaking at the Yale Divinity School, I referred to gay people, along with other creative minorities struggling for human justice, as a new Moral Minority. When I addressed a meeting of Presbyterians for Lesbian/Gay Concerns at the 196th General Assembly of the Presbyterian Church (U.S.A.), I criticized religious enemies of gay people who seek to appropriate the words *family values* to their exclusive use. I explained that Jesus, a single adult, came from a family and belonged to an extended family. All gays come from families, and many live in extended families.

Preaching to nearly a thousand people who packed a cathedral in Vancouver, British Columbia, during the third Gay Olympics, I happily affirmed, "Thank God I am gay!" Invited to speak during the twentieth anniversary celebration of the Universal Fellowship of Metropolitan Community Churches (MCC), I said, "Gay and lesbian spirituality and theology will build a bridge between this present time and the post-AIDS era. It will transform the face of theology as we know it." One way is the demythologizing of death and the remythologizing of life.

At a conference on gay spirituality in Berkeley, California, sponsored by the River Zen Group and the Tayu Center for Gay Spirituality, I said that as gays we need to claim God and morality rather than let either be used oppressively against us and that we must have the courage to create our own theology. Preaching in Grace Cathedral, San Francisco, at the fifteenth anniversary of the founding of Integrity, the Episcopal gay and lesbian caucus, I referred to "a breakthrough" that had taken place: "Lesbians and gay men are right to require the church to honor our lives and relationships. But instead of waiting for their approval, we must achieve our own solutions and live out our own destiny."

I feel that I have done this in my own life. Time is too sacred to waste. The years, months, weeks, days, and hours are both precious and blessed. I can't wait laboriously for other people to come up with solutions for my life. Celebrating and honoring my life—and giving God genuine thanks for it—I must live it as fully, honestly, joyfully, and responsibly as I can. This means *living* it—not in a dank dungeon of denial but in the light of God's freedom.

As I write this, my seventieth birthday is around the corner. I await the year 2000, with the emergence of a new century. I want to meet it with an open heart and a naked face.